Trinnacle Rocks, Dovestones, Saddleworth Moor.

Visitor's Guide *The British Isles*

3

Published by Visitor's Guide Ltd
World Leisure Marketing Ltd
Unit 11, Newmarket Court
Newmarket Drive
Derby DE24 8NW
Tel: 01332 573737
Fax: 01332 573399
E-mail: office@wlmsales.co.uk

ISBN 1 84006 022 0

British Library Cataloguing in Publication Data:
A catalogue record for this book is available from the British Library

Production and design by Isabelle Lewis
Editorial and proof reading by Kay Coulson
Maps: © Using information from Bartholomew mapping base.
Reproduced with permission of HarperCollins Publishers Ltd. MM-0798-192.

Colour origination by GA Graphics, Stamford, UK
Printed in China by Midas Printing (HK)Ltd
The paper used in this book originates from sustainable sources
and is totally chlorine free.

The contents of this book are believed correct at the time of printing.
Nevertheless, the publishers and the author cannot be held responsible for any errors or
omissions or for changes in the details given in this book or for the consequences of
any reliance on the information provided.

About the author

Brian was introduced to his love of the Peak District by his paternal
grandparents who recounted stories about lead mining and life on the High
Peak Railway, and also about the arduous, yet happy life as a worker in
Arkwright's Cromford Mill. A freelance writer on outdoor topics, Brian's home
is in the Peak District, where he has served as an appointed member of the
Peak District National Park Authority.

The
Peak District

How to use this guide

Over 50 suggested walks are highlighted in yellow throughout this
guide and are described
in detail in the section starting
on p 156

The author's special
recommendations are in bold in the
text with extra information in a
green box

*Additional background information
is in pale yellow next to the text*

Maps are located at the beginning of each chapter.
For walking reference refer to:
Ordnance Survey maps, available from all good bookshops
or from Travellers World Bookshop:
Tel: 0800 838080 (quote reference VGPD)

Brian Spencer

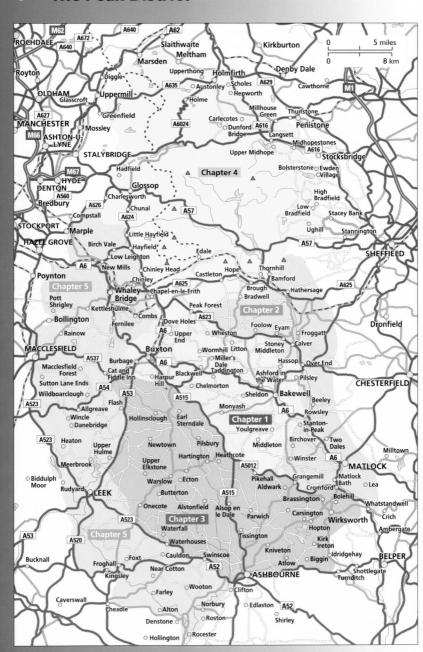

Contents 5

1. Caudwell's Mill, Rowsley .

2. Chatsworth from the river

3. Tissington Hall.

4. The eastern edges.

5. Lyme Hall in spring.

Key to all maps

river/lake		700m/2300ft
≡11≡ motorway	small roads	500m/1640ft
A roads	railway	300m/985ft
B roads	▲ peak	0m/ft

About this guide

T This guide is an exploration of the Peak District National Park and its immediate surroundings. It is designed to help first time visitors as well as those with a wider knowledge of the area, discover or rediscover, the many and varied faces of its delightful countryside. The guide points the reader towards not only the renowned attractions of the Peak, but helps find those out of the way and generally little visited corners.

Top left: Stanage Edge.
Bottom left: Bradford Dale.
Top right: Ilam Rock, Dovedale.
Middle: Children at the National Stone Centre, Wirksworth.
Left: Garland King in Castleton.

The National Trust owns and maintains parts of the Peak.

The area covered by this guide

As well as attractions in and around the wild moorlands of the Dark Peak, and the gentler uplands and dales of the White Peak, many places described in this guide lie in comparatively unfrequented side valleys surrounding the Peak District National Park. The beautiful countryside of the Peak District does not end at the boundary of the national park and because of this, the area covered by the guide is roughly that shown on the Ordnance Survey one inch Tourist Map of the Peak District, but with the addition of the Staffordshire Moorlands and its little known Churnet Valley to the south west. Careful restoration of one-time mill workers' cottages in hamlets and towns beyond the northern limits of the national park warrant their inclusion, while to the east and south, high ground has created a natural buffer zone where many of the villages once played a part in important historical events.

How the Peak was made

Its pre-history – With few exceptions, the countryside we see and enjoy today is man made. However, no matter what man does to the environment, good or bad, that work is controlled by the natural shape of the land and in turn determined by the rocks beneath the ground.

The rocks which created the shape and vegetation of the Peak were laid down between 325 and 360 million years ago far away to the south of their present site. Peakland limestone, now much in demand for road stone, is made from the remains of countless billions of plants and animals once living in a tropical sea. This sea with its surrounding lagoons and coral reefs was occasionally disturbed by small volcanoes. Lava from them can still be seen as outcrops such as in Tideswell Dale; the Peak even has its own minuscule version of the Giant's Causeway at the top of Cave Dale above Castleton.

Rock climbing on the gritstone edges.

At some point in time a massive river delta dumped the sandy remains of an even older mountain range from a long disappeared continent to the north. This sand and mud began to settle, turning gradually into the dark gritstone which now outcrops on the northern moors and abrupt escarpment edges high above the main valleys.

Starting as horizontal layers, both the limestone and gritstones became contorted by later earth movements. Minor cracks or faults allowed minerals, predominantly lead, to force their way towards the surface, laying down riches for future exploitation.* Calcium fluoride, fluorspa, once ignored by the old lead miners is now a valued source of the chemical fluorine.

* Many of the lead-filled cracks, they are known as rakes in the Peak, can be traced by lines of trees planted not just as wind breaks, but to prevent cattle grazing on the old spoil heaps and developing a disease known in Derbyshire as 'beland.'

Gradually over millions of years pressures from deep within the earth moved the land masses towards their present continental sites. At the same time what eventually became the Peak District was lifted into a massive dome thousands of feet high, inter-cut by the forerunners of today's network of valleys and dales. Climatic changes first created desert conditions, but none were more dramatic than the series of glaciers of the Ice Ages which scoured and honed the rocks into their present form. It was during this stage that the only true peaks of the Peak District were shaped. Chrome and Parkhouse hills, the remnants of ancient coral reefs, and gritstone-based Shutlingsloe and Win Hill are the only recognisably pointed summits in the Peak. The name Peak has been around a long time and comes from the Old English 'peac', and simply means a 'hill'. In the Anglo-Saxon Chronicle of AD 924, the area was known as Peaclond.

When the ice eventually melted, vast quantities of water scoured the valleys, dissolving underlying limestone to create a network of caves and pot holes throughout what is now known as the White Peak.

Man in the landscape

Early Man – As the last Ice Age began its final retreat about ten thousand years ago, tundra-like vegetation colonised a landscape roamed by mammoths, reindeer, wild ox, wolves, bears and other exotic wildlife. The first visitors to the Peak District were migrant hunters who came annually from warmer southern areas, using for primitive shelter caves such as Thor's and Ossom's in the Manifold Valley. Here archaeologists have discovered primitive flint scrapers, while arrow heads can be found in the gravel of moorland streams.

With continuing milder weather, the first Neolithic settlers were able to move into the Peak about five thousand years ago. These people were the forerunners of a mainly Celtic population who led a remarkably sophisticated way of life, but regrettably left no complete understanding of their customs. Living in circular hutted communities, they were great movers of stone and built henges of locally found materials such as the gritstone circle of Nine Ladies on Stanton Moor, or the massive ring of limestone slabs at

Arbor Low. Unique in that its stones are recumbent, Arbor Low is considered almost as important as Stonehenge. Along with erecting stone circles, these people also buried their dead on wind-swept hill tops beneath the huge mounds we now call *tumuli*.

Top: Weird gritstone shapes contrast with the tranquility of the dales (above).

As the technology of our early ancestors developed, leading to what has been termed first the Bronze then later the Iron Ages, they created a network of trackways linking their more important sites. One of these tracks is the Portway which ran from the Trent Valley to the Iron Age fort on Mam Tor and can still be traced by modern paths and roads, and placenames.

Why or with what means Iron Age people built the huge ramparts of their fort on the bleak summit of Mam Tor, or moved huge boulders to fortify Carl Wark is open to conjecture. By their very size the forts would have been difficult to defend and even though they were built before the Romans occupied northern England, there is no hint or record of any siege taking place. Modern thought suggests that rather than being simply military forts, many also had some religious purpose.

The Roman Invaders – The main reason the Romans came to the Peak District was to exploit its mineral riches. Lead and to a lesser degree silver, had been mined by the locals for centuries. The Romans with their insatiable demand for lead for plumbing and roofing soon subjugated the Peakland tribes and if folklore is correct, used them as slave labour in the mines around present day Bradwell and Middleton-by-Wirksworth. Establishing their forts at strategic sites throughout the Peak they linked them by a system of roads frequently following the line of pre-historic trackways. The modern A515 for example, still follows long stretches of a Roman road, which in turn had been built along an ancient Celtic track. In Roman times this road, still known in places as 'The Street', linked the centre of their lead mining activities, *Lutudaron*, currently thought to have been near Carsington and *Aquae Arnemetiae*, modern Buxton.

Dene Quarry, Cromford. Quarrying is an important industry in the Peak.

Controlling the sparsely populated region of mostly Brigantian tribes by a policy of 'divide and rule', the Romans held a firm grip on the Peak. Discovering a source of thermally heated water dedicated to the Celtic water goddess *Santan*, they built an elaborate system of baths and called the town that developed around it, *Aquae Arnemetiae*, one of only two Roman towns honoured with the pre-fix *Aquae*; the other being *Aquae Sulis*, Bath.*****

* It is interesting to note that the present source of thermal water in Buxton is dedicated to St Ann, a Christianisation of the Celtic goddess Santan. No doubt the locals reverted to the original name once the Romans left.

After the Norman Conquest – With the departure of the Romans, the country slipped into anarchy, but gradually over the years some form of stability grew. Land hungry raiders from across the North Sea, first Saxon then Danish came and gradually settled, mixing with the local Celts. Christianity took over from the pagan beliefs, frequently assimilating ancient customs, many of which still remain. Little is left of the first churches built by missionaries, but numbers of exquisitely carved Saxon preaching crosses still adorn Peakland churchyards.

The peaceful way of life enjoyed in Anglo-Saxon times was soon to vanish, following the quarrel between King Harold of England and William Duke of Normandy over who was the rightful heir to the English throne.

The knights of William the Conqueror supported him in 1066 on the understanding they would be given properties in the newly subjugated territories. However, all did not go well for them, despite their victory over the exhausted forces of King Harold at the Battle of Hastings. Saxon settlers in northern England did not willingly accept their new rulers and were frequently in rebellion. In order to sort matters out William sent his troops northwards through the East Midlands, killing everyone they came across, and burning all the farms and villages. One of the results of this unprecedented slaughter was a huge reduction in the amount of taxes paid to the crown. In the *Domesday* survey of 1086, the expression *Wassa Est* - 'All is Waste' , occurs time after time against Peakland entries. Once prosperous villages had disappeared, ethnically cleansed by rampaging Norman troops.

Norman knights had a great love for the chase and created royal hunting forests throughout their new kingdom. Much of the Peak was ideal for this purpose: Peak Forest was bounded by the rivers Goyt, Etherow and Derwent; Macclesfield Forest lands can still be traced from place names in and around Wildboarclough, but Malbanc Forest to the west of Dovedale is now virtually unknown. Protected by harsh laws, most of the high ground in the Peak was reserved for hunting and William Peveril founded the fortress, which still dominates the village of Castleton, partly to control lead mining interests but mainly as a royal hunting lodge.

Agricultural lands of the more fertile White Peak were divided amongst the monasteries. Although no abbeys were built in the Peak, monastic farms were created, still bearing the title 'Grange' as part of their name.

Top: Chelmorton's preserved medieval field pattern. Above: Local markets such as this one in Wirksworth are an essential part of Peakland life.

Medieval times and later – Until the dissolution of the monasteries by Henry VIII, the pattern of land ownership in the Peak was mostly controlled by the abbeys. It was a time of agricultural expansion with much of the wool-based wealth used to build superbly designed churches; in particular Tideswell parish church which quite rightly enjoys the title of the 'Cathedral of the Peak'. Markets developed together with fairs and the first recorded was Tideswell's in 1251, which is still celebrated as the annual 'wakes'.

Land owned by the monasteries was shared amongst Henry's knights and courtiers, the founders of many of the Peak's noble families. Generation after generation used the wealth from their land ownership to improve their homes. Chatsworth for example, grew from a simple Tudor manor house into the magnificent Palladian palace begun by the first Duke of Devonshire in 1687. Lancelot 'Capability' Brown was commissioned to landscape the grounds even though this meant the disappearance of villages recorded in the *Domesday Book*. The Legh family built Lyme Hall in the 18th century. Designed by Leoni it replaced a Tudor and Jacobean hall and though slightly smaller than Chatsworth, it is no less a magnificent building. Local squires were still able to expand their properties, building Tissington Hall, Hartington Hall, North Lees and many others during a time when land ownership meant wealth.

Lead mining, controlled by Barmote Courts to oversee fair play,***** became established as the major Peakland industry as early as Saxon times, and it helped develop the fortunes of major landowners, in particular the Dukes of Devonshire and Rutland who built palaces with their lead mining income.

* Wirksworth's Barmote Court still meets each year on the third Wednesday in April.

Mary Queen of Scots' captivity in the Peak – The Scots' queen, a thorn in the side of Tudor Queen Elizabeth, was placed in captivity into the hands of the trusted Earl of Shrewsbury, owner of several properties in and around Derbyshire. During this time Mary Queen of Scots became good friends with the Earl's wife, the Countess of Shrewsbury, better known as Bess of Hardwick. Both were expert needleworkers and many examples of their work still survive. All that is left of the Tudor version of Chatsworth which held the queen, is the raised garden close to the old bridge where she spent many happy hours. Constantly on the move in all weathers between the Earl's Derbyshire properties, the queen developed rheumatism and to help ease the pain she made frequent visits to Buxton's thermal spa waters, staying each time at what became the Old Hall Hotel.

Transport networks – the state of Peakland roads, which had been well maintained in Roman times, deteriorated throughout the Middle Ages. Even as late as the 17th century travellers such as the indefatigable Celia Fiennes and author Daniel Defoe complained about the state of the roads. Conditions were so bad that simple cross-Peak journeys often required guides.

With the expansion of the population, the first reasonable tracks were developed by packhorse traders. Trains of sturdy ponies carried an amazing variety of goods, ranging from fish to stone, but the major trade was carrying salt from Cheshire and wool to the textile manufacturing centres, with finished cloth carried on the return journey.

Gradually things improved with the coming of the turnpike era when acts of Parliament ensured that roads were properly maintained. Mailcoaches, romantic to our modern eyes, crossed the Peak in all weathers, keeping to very tight schedules. Better roads allowed heavier loads of goods to be carried and soon the jingle of pack ponies was overtaken by the creak of wheeled vehicles.

The canal network, despite its efficiency over road-borne goods, never fully penetrated the Peak. Canals were planned, there was even an audacious scheme to build a canal via Matlock and Bakewell and the Edale valley to link with the Peak Forest Canal at its Bugsworth (Buxworth), basin. Mountainous terrain and lack of water on the limestone uplands of the White Peak prevented the building of a direct link between the steadily growing industrial centres of Manchester and Nottingham. In 1832 that important link was created when the Cromford and High Peak Railway joined the Cromford Canal to that of Peak Forest at Whaley Bridge. Built by canal engineers the railway climbed steep inclines, assisted by steam driven winches, very much as a canal would cross the countryside.*

* The High Peak Railway is now preserved for much of its length as a cycle and pedestrian trail, where the remains of stations are still called wharves.

Much faster and able to carry greater loads than barges, railways soon overtook canals. The Midland Railway, built to connect Manchester, the East Midlands and London was planned to follow the Derwent Valley, but when it reached Rowsley in 1849 the company had to face the intransigencies of both the Duke of Devonshire and the Duke of Rutland. Neither duke would allow the line to spoil their parkland and as a result, for several years Rowsley was the northern terminus of the Midland Line. A compromise was eventually reached when the railway was tunnelled beneath Haddon Hall before starting the long and arduous climb through Monsal Dale. Not satisfied with redirecting the line, both dukes insisted on being provided with grandiose stations, at Bakewell and Hassop. The line north of Matlock was closed under the Beeching Axe in the 1960s. Now known as the Monsal Trail, the Bakewell to Miller's Dale section of the track is used as a walkers' and cyclists' path, but if the efforts of the voluntary-run Peak Rail Society come to fruition, maybe one day huge maroon-liveried steam locomotives will once again haul their way along the almost alpine line.

Many lives were lost, mostly through cholera, when the Woodhead Tunnel was built to take the Manchester, Penistone, Sheffield line beneath the northern moors. This line is closed and the tunnel abandoned, but the other major railway undertaking, that linking Sheffield and Manchester via the Edale valley still functions, offering good links with towns and villages of the Dark Peak.

The Industrial Revolution – Stocking knitting was once an important cottage industry in villages around the southern boundary of the Peak. Richard Arkwright (1732-1792), searching for suitable sites to build a water powered spinning mill, developed Cromford as the first completely independent factory village. Other mills soon followed, using the readily available power of local rivers, often in almost inaccessible valleys. With the coming of steam power, gradually many of these mills were abandoned, some preserved by conversion into modern flats or industrial units, but the links the Peak District had with the Industrial Revolution never expanded beyond its early roots.

Top: examples of Well Dressing. Skills are handed down through the generations. Above: The painstaking work of filling the intricate patterns.

Peakland customs and festivals

Many Peakland customs and festivals are unique to the area, often Christianised versions of pagan Celtic rites. That most famous of all festivals celebrated in the Peak, Well Dressing, is an ancient offering of thanks for the supply of water in the predominantly dry limestone uplands. Originally this was the simple offering of floral tributes to the local well but in its present form boards covered with a layer of damp clay depict scenes and patterns made from flower petals, mosses and twigs. Every village taking part in this custom has its own jealously guarded version and designs worked out in the dark winter months are not revealed until the last possible moment.

Every 29th May, the villagers of Castleton dress a man in Jacobean costume with a cone of flowers covering him from his head almost to his waist. Ostensibly celebrating the restoration of King Charles II in 1660, the Garland festival is quite possibly the modern equivalent of an ancient fertility rite.

Ashbourne shopkeepers board their windows and traffic comes to a halt at Shrovetide, for this is when the two halves of the town enjoy a 'no holds barred' game of football. *

Far gentler, but still with pre-Christian links is the delightful practice of 'Clypping', where Wirksworth parishioners holding hands surround the churchyard. A little later in its origins is the custom of spreading rushes on the floor of the tiny Forest Chapel in Wildboarclough or the now abandoned but not forgotten Ashford and Matlock church custom of hanging paper garlands, Shakespeare's 'virgin crants', in memory of girls who died before marriage. The Love Feast held in a tiny barn in the remote Alport Valley below Bleaklow, continues a festival begun by religiously oppressed non-conformists in the eighteenth century.

On mid-summer's eve modern followers of ancient pagan beliefs have been seen celebrating within the confines of stone circles on Stanton Moor, in their way keeping alive what they consider to be ageless practices. Hardier souls join the Boxing Day raft race in Matlock. Bonsall is noted for the almost lifelike quality of its Bonfire Night Guy Fawkes dummies, while nearby Winster keeps the traditions of Morris Dancing alive in summer, and in winter Guisers visit pubs and houses in the surrounding area, performing their strange pantomime. Winster also celebrates Shrove Tuesday with pancake races in the village main street.

* The only difference between the modern version of Shrovetide football and that played by their Celtic forefathers, is that a specially made ball is used in place of a human head!

How to find things to do

Organised activities and events throughout the Peak District are regularly advertised in the national park free newspaper *Peakland Post,* along with *Summertime*, a guide to tourism, leisure and shopping in Derbyshire, and also in local newspapers or magazines such as the *Peakland Advertiser, Peak and Pennine* and *Derbyshire Life*. Further up-to-date details can be found at information centres throughout the area. See page 185 for addresses.

Cycle hire centres (addresses page 180), are mostly conveniently sited near traffic-free trails and have bicycles suitable for all age groups and abilities.

Boat hire and tuition is offered on Carsington Water (address page 174), where there is also a safe cycle-and walk-way.

Public transport is fairly good in the Peak District. *The Derbyshire Wayfarer* ticket allows a day's unlimited travel on all local buses throughout the county, and also travel to and from Sheffield, Macclesfield, Leek, Uttoxeter and Burton. Timetables and maps of all bus and train routes are included in the *Peak District Timetable Book*, available at Bus Stations, Tourist Information Centres and Libraries throughout Derbyshire.

The Peak District National Park

Once travel became relatively easy, the countryside bounded by the industrial centres of the north Midlands became a place for recreation and enjoyment. With roughly half of the population of England living within less than an hour's journey from the Peak District, visitor pressure soon became a problem.

In the 1920s and 30s city dwellers and factory workers looked to the hills and moors for respite against the humdrum life of their working week. Often protected by armed gamekeepers, the moors were the preserve of their grouse shooting owners. In the wake of unemployment, political awareness encouraged many walkers to take things into their own hands in the demand for access to the moors. Protest rallies were organised of little or no avail, but things came to a head on 24th April 1932 when the now celebrated Mass Trespass on to Kinder Scout was staged. With their plans well publicised in advance, the trespassers were met by groups of gamekeepers stationed along the escarpment lip above William Clough. Scuffles broke out and as a result six ramblers were arrested and charged with riotous assembly and assault, five of them receiving between two and six months jail sentences at Derby Assizes.

The need for the Mass Trespass has since been questioned, but whatever the rights or wrongs of such action it became one of the catalysts of legislation aimed at the creation of National Parks and access to the countryside. In 1947 the National Parks Committee led by Sir Arthur Hobhouse recommended the Peak District as one of the National Parks in England and Wales. Only four years elapsed between this recommendation and the Peak District becoming the first National Park in 1951. Unlike National Parks in the USA and other countries, the land is mostly privately owned, the workplace and home of local people.

One of the first tasks the newly fledged Peak District National Park gave itself was to negotiate access to

the moors and other semi-wilderness areas. As a result ramblers can now roam freely on upwards of 76 square miles of northern and eastern moorland, including Kinder Scout, scene of the Mass Trespass. The only restrictions are that the moors are closed during times of high fire risk, or when grouse-shooting takes place. Prior to the 1997 Labour Government's pledge to legislate for easier access to open spaces, access land in the Peak accounted for about 60 per cent of the total in England and Wales.

Now a constituted authority, the Peak District National Park is administered by a committee of representatives of local county, district and parish councils, as well as up to a third of its members being appointed for their specific knowledge of the area by the Secretary of State for the Environment. The prime duty of the authority is basically to protect the natural beauty of the landscape and its wildlife, whether it be the bleak moorland of the Dark Peak, or the sylvan glories of Dovedale. Despite the pressures of modern farming techniques, dry stone walls delineating ancient field patterns and wild flowered hay meadows also need to be preserved. Carefully monitored planning controls ensure that building development blends sympathetically with traditional styles of architecture.

**Left: Winster Guisers perform in local pubs and homes at Christmas.
Right: Winster Pancake Races.**

Footpath maintenance and signposting is a very important feature of access to the countryside.

Top: The art of stone
wall building is very
much alive in the Peak.
Above: Young cows are
often curious of
passing walkers.

An insatiable requirement for roadstone makes great demands on the Peak's major natural resource, limestone. Unfortunately this commodity seems to occur mostly in National Parks and as a result, ugly quarries mar sections of the White Peak landscape. *

Bearing in mind that the Peak National Park is a landscape where its inhabitants must make a living, a number of industrial developments have been created which sympathetically blend into the environment. Industries ranging from the highly successful baker of oatcakes, a northern delicacy, to the mono-culture of plants, can be found in small estates in villages such as Longnor or Tideswell. David Mellor's cutlery works pleasingly breaks with tradition within a circular factory built on the site of an abandoned gasometer near Hathersage.

* Opencast mining of fluorspa, a material ignored by ancient lead miners, provides the raw material for fluorine, used in products as diverse as toothpaste, PVC plastic, non-stick coatings for pans and as a flux to purify steel. Strictly controlled, quarry owners are under constant pressure to minimise the impact of their excavations.

Visitor services

One of the obligations of National Parks is to provide a Ranger Service, acting as a link between locals and visitors. Their duties range from rescuing crag-fast sheep, rebuilding drystone walls, fighting moorland fires, assisting volunteers working on footpath restoration, to building stiles and all too often co-ordinating searches for missing walkers.

Innovative traffic-free schemes in the Goyt Valley and Upper Derwent mean that visitors can enjoy these remote valleys without the problems of traffic congestion. During summer weekends and Bank Holidays, regular bus services passing conveniently sited car parks as well as cycle hire, help everyone to reach normally inaccessible places without the use of cars.

Other easy walking or cycling can be found on trails based on old railways, such as Longdendale, Sett Valley, High Peak, Monsal and Tissington Trails. The trails are also suitable for horse riding, especially beginners.

For those visitors who want to find out more about the Peak District National Park, there are a number of information centres throughout the park and Losehill Hall Study Centre offers day or residential courses covering a wide range of subjects.

The Derbyshire Wye and Lathkill Dale

Bounding the limestone plateau of the White Peak, the River Wye begins its short life in Buxton. Here a series of peaty moorland streams join, then flow eastwards through some of the finest limestone gorges in the country, before turning south east between watermeadows on either side of Ashford in the Water and Bakewell. Offering a tree-shaded foreground to Haddon Hall, the river is soon joined by sylvan River Lathkill, where the blended waters meander onwards, linking with the Derwent at Rowsley.

Caudwell's Mill in Rowsley.

The Crescent in Buxton was built by the 5th Duke of Devonshire.

High above the valleys, tiny unspoilt villages dot the limestone uplands, fitting inside a triangle created by the A6, A515 and A5012, the major arterial roads to cross the White Peak. Dairy cattle graze lush meadow grasses on the thin but rich soil of farms scattered across a breezy landscape. Lead miners no longer eke a meagre income from beneath the green rolling meadows, but many of their former homes remain, fitting snugly into the timeless scene. In sharp contrast with the upland hamlets, bustling Bakewell, market town for the south of the Peak, still retains much of its medieval atmosphere, despite the pressures of tourism and commerce.

Buxton, keeps the best of its Victorian spa-town layout, especially around the town centre, managing to ignore the massive limestone quarries on its outskirts. The town can trace its roots to the Celts who discovered thermally heated water and dedicated the flow to their goddess *Santan*. Later this well provided warm water for a Roman bath built to cleanse troops garrisoning the nearby fort of *Aquae Arnemetiae*, thought to lie underneath Buxton market place. Heated to a constant 28°C (82°F), deep within the earth, the waters have never failed and from medieval times onward, people came to Buxton on pilgrimage. Dedicated to *St Ann*, a

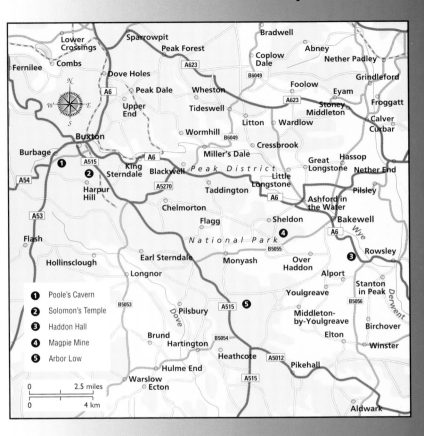

Map legend:
1. Poole's Cavern
2. Solomon's Temple
3. Haddon Hall
4. Magpie Mine
5. Arbor Low

Christianised version of the Celtic name, at one time the well was thought to have miraculous powers, but Henry VIII ordered it to be closed.

The development of modern Buxton began with the fashion of 'taking the waters' in the eighteenth century. Using profits from his copper mines at Ecton Hill in the Manifold Valley, the 5th Duke of Devonshire planned a northern version of Bath. As the centre piece of his grand design, he appointed the architect John Carr of York to build the splendid Crescent which originally contained three hotels and several baths. Failing with the decline of spas, the Crescent fell into disrepair in the last decade or so, but is presently undergoing a

Above and below, the massively domed Devonshire Hospital in Buxton.

* A short queue of devotees can usually be seen waiting their turn to collect the free spa water flowing constantly from St Ann's Well.

programme of restoration. Arcaded shops now fill the space where once bathers eased their rheumatic limbs, with high quality housing and hotels planned for the main building.

* Behind St Ann's Well and opposite the Crescent, graded paths once tested the benefits of the water cure. They were laid out on the grassy slope by Sir Jeffry Wyatville in 1811, who also designed the elegant parish church behind the Crescent.

Opposite the church the circular dome-roofed **Devonshire Hospital** was originally a riding school, built in 1790. The central part was uncovered and used for riding practice with stables and grooms' rooms in the surrounding area. In 1858 the 6th Duke converted half of the building into a hospital and then in 1880 the circular central space was covered with what is still the world's largest unsupported dome, with a span of 154ft.

Railways reached Buxton in 1863 and marked the zenith of its popularity as a health resort. Along with visitors from far and wide it became fashionable for Manchester textile barons' families to move in for the 'season', with fathers commuting over the weekend. The stately Palace Hotel was built about this time to accommodate the increased numbers of visitors and to entertain them; the **Pavilion** and its still attractive **riverside gardens** was built in 1871.

Buxton Pavilion Gardens, open daily, all year.

Of all the buildings from this bygone era, the ornate **Opera House** which was opened in 1905, still evokes an 18th-century elegance. Throughout the year, concerts and plays with well known visiting performers are staged, along with a traditional pantomime every Christmas; Gilbert and Sullivan productions as well as festivals are now a regular feature. Buxton and its Opera House host the now internationally renowned Buxton Festival of Music and the Arts.

Buxton's history from the dawn of time almost to the present day is explained in the award winning **Museum and Art Gallery** near the market place. Dioramas, complete with sound effects, graphically bring back the time of the dinosaurs. Along with archaeological remains and fine examples of objects made of local marble and Blue John, the study of the local philosopher, Sir William Boyd-Dawkins has been recreated as it would have looked a hundred years or so ago.

Buxton Museum and Art Gallery. Local history and works of art.

Spring Gardens, Buxton's main shopping street is now mostly pedestrianised, and has a pleasing mix of multiple and family-run stores, and cafés. Regular Wednesday and Saturday markets are held at the top of the hill above the town centre, where there are more shops. *

Poole's Cavern on the south-western outskirts of the town was the reputed home of an outlaw, but was certainly lived in by Romano-Celtic man. Now a show cave, it has many interesting formations and is suitable for all ages and abilities, but wheelchair users will need assistance.

* Winters can be quite harsh in Buxton with heavy snowfalls. Canadian soldiers garrisoned there at the end of the first World War, built a toboggan run, now known as the Cresta Run on Burbage golf course. Quite exciting when the snow is just right, it can be found on the left immediately beyond the last houses as you leave Buxton on the A5002.

The cavern is just one of the features of **Grin Low Country Park** where species of wild plants such as field orchids can be found, making it a Site of Special Scientific Interest (S.S.S.I.). A walk through Grinlow

Solomon's Temple Walk p 157

Solomon's Temple.

(1) Solomon's Temple is a Victorian folly, built in 1896 to provide work for unemployed quarrymen. It stands on the site of a Bronze Age burial mound, or tumulus.

* (2) No longer does the shriek and thunder of trains echo along the valley sides, prompting the Victorian environmentalist, John Ruskin to comment; 'The valley is gone and the gods with it, and now every fool in Buxton can be at Bakewell in half an hour and every fool in Bakewell at Buxton; which you think a lucrative process of exchange - you Fools everywhere'.

Woods leads to **Solomon's Temple**.*(1) The climb to the tower only takes about 20 minutes and is well worth the effort, if only to enjoy the wide ranging views. Don't worry if you hear explosions coming from the group of buildings on the hillside to your left. They will be coming from the Explosion and Fire Laboratory of the Health and Safety Executive, where they have even been known to assess the explosive characteristics of custard powder!

The laboratory is within the confines of Harpur Hill Industrial Estate where the Go-Karting Centre's track is alongside a 4x4 circuit and skid pan. Advanced driving courses are also provided. Frequent banger race meets are held throughout the year on High Edge which is immediately above the estate. Access is from the narrow minor road south east of the A53 at Axe Edge.

The A6 road follows the Wye through deep and narrow Ashwood Dale, sharing its wooded confines with the railway as far as Topley Pike. The road climbs the pike to a layby viewpoint overlooking Tunstead Quarry, I.C.I's huge limestone operation. Fortunately much of the largest hole in Europe is hidden within Great Rocks Dale, and hardly detracts from the delightful upland scenery.

A side road on the left, the B6049, leads downhill past Blackwell hamlet where the squire forfeited his lands through supporting the wrong side in the Civil War. In the valley bottom, tiny **Miller's Dale** once echoed to the hiss and clank of trains linking Buxton to the London/Manchester Midland Line. Such was the volume of traffic along this section of line that two viaducts had to be built across the Wye.*(2) Now part of the **Monsal Trail**, the abandoned track is used as a walkers' and cyclists' path, linked with many of the rights of way along the valley.

Not only can walkers and cyclists enjoy the amenity of a high-level traffic-free path along the trail, but anyone with even the slightest interest in geology will be able to search for fossils exposed along the cuttings left by the Victorian railway navigators. A little above and to the side of the track beyond Miller's Dale viaduct, the preserved limekilns of an abandoned quarry and its exposed rocks are explained by easily understood plaques. A haven of wildflowers, the quarry and Priestcliffe Lees above is designated as a National Nature Reserve.

Corn is no longer milled in Miller's Dale. The old mill is now used by a woodworkers and craft supplies company who also run wood turning and carving as well as lace making holiday courses.

A walk between Miller's Dale Station and Monk's Dale by way of Wormhill is an ideal way to explore this little known corner. **Wormhill**, directly above luxuriant Chee Dale is a quiet sheltered hamlet where change is slow and placid; the church is 700 years old, while the village stocks have not been used for over a century. James Brindley the canal builder was born here in 1716, a plaque marks the site of the house. Almost opposite is a hiker-friendly café and guest house.

Top: Miller's Dale.
Above: Monsal Dale.

Miller's Dale Walk
p 157

The walk avoids the confines of rocky Monk's Dale by following farm lanes to its east. **Monk's Dale**, a National Nature Reserve, is part of a six mile long dry dale between Peak Forest and Miller's Dale. Changing its name four times, the dale is first Dam Dale, then becomes Hay Dale, Peter Dale and Monk's Dale in that

Miller's Dale and Monk's Dale National Nature Reserves

The 'Cathedral of the Peak', Tideswell's magnificent parish church.

order. Only densely wooded Monk's Dale is difficult to follow, and in fact there is a right of way along it, but throughout spring and early summer wild flowers bloom in profusion. Masses of early purple and spotted orchids can be found in the comparatively treeless sections, and though rare through over picking in the past, the pure white bells and heady scent of lily-of-the-valley delight the senses.

Wheston north-west of Tideswell, is mostly farms dating mainly from the 17th and 18th centuries, clustered around a 15th-century village cross, unusually within a small enclosure.

Tideswell sits in the bottom of a shallow bowl, sheltered from winter winds by the surrounding high ground. Almost a small town, it is one of the most self-supporting places in the Peak. A well-designed industrial estate provides employment for many of the locals and a good range of shops has prevented Tideswell from becoming a dormitory. Visitors will be attracted to its excellent range of pubs and small restaurants, but the church is its pride and joy. Rightly known as the '**Cathedral of the Peak**', it dates from the 14th-century, and despite a forced break while the Black Death raged, it is an indication of the wool-based wealth at that time; decorated mainly by 19th-century Suffolk carvers and a local man Advent Hunstone, whose nephew still follows the family tradition. The history of Tideswell is written amongst the ornate tombstones, for here are buried local worthies such as the Foljambes; Robert Pursglove was like the Vicar of Bray who in the 16th century moved from Protestant to Papist at the dictates of changing monarchic styles.*

The ebbing and flowing well which gave Tideswell its name and was once called one of the Seven Wonders of the Peak, was in the garden of the house known as 'Welyards'. Even though the garden is open on advertised days, it is no use looking for the well as it has been dry since piped water was introduced to the village. The village wells are dressed for the annual wakes week beginning on the Saturday nearest to St John the Baptist Day. (See the *Peakland Post* and other local publications for the exact date.)

Tucked away along a side road is **Litton**, Tideswell's near neighbour; a pleasant group of limestone cottages and one pub around a tiny village green. A useful starting point for local walks, it dresses its wells in the same week as Tideswell.

A footpath runs along **Tideswell Dale** which when linked to other local paths, makes an ideal way to explore the roadless and most beautiful part of the Wye between Miller's Dale and Monsal Head. Access to Tideswell Dale starts at the car park beside the B6049, and shortly passes an old quarry where dolerite, a form of volcanic basalt was worked. Ahead are the limestone ramparts of Raven's Tor, whose river-facing walls are the haunt of rock climbers. The summit of the crag Tongue End, is almost an alpine meadow enjoyed by those who stay at the nearby youth hostel.

In the valley bottom a narrow, almost traffic-free road, leads downstream to **Litton Mill**. Using the power of the Wye from 1782 until it ceased producing textiles in the 1960s, Litton Mill has a tragic history. Run by virtual slave labour, it employed orphan and pauper children who fell into the dubious care of the 'Guardians of the Poor'. These 'do-gooders' of their day, eased the strain on local rates in places as far away as London by farming out their charges to whoever wanted cheap labour. Cruelly treated and fed on

* William Newton, the Minstrel of the Peak is commemorated by a sundial. He once owned nearby Cressbrook Mill; a rarity in his day, for his pauper employees were better treated than most.

Tideswell Well Dressing
Held each year in June.

Tideswell Dale Walk
p 158

(1) Robert Blincoe who experienced the dreadful conditions at Litton Mill, wrote a book about his life there in the early part of the 19th century.

meagre rations, the children worked a 15 hour day, six days a week, living in an overcrowded barracks beyond the main part of the mill. Records of the numbers who died were carefully hidden by arranging for victims to be buried well away from the mill.*(1) Neglected for several years, the fabric of the mill has deteriorated in recent years, and even a proposal to convert the building into holiday flats including accommodation for the disabled, seems, at the time of writing this guide, to have come to a stop.

The dale below Litton Mill is completely traffic free and only pedestrians can enjoy its hidden delights. Water-cum-Jolly is the name given to this pretty section of dale, overhung by sheer limestone crags on one side, and a steep grassy hillside the other. The tranquil scene is completed by a widening of the river, created from a stroke of innocent genius to power a water wheel which once drove **Cressbrook Mill**. The main part of the present mill dates from 1815 and was once owned by the father of the factory system, Sir Richard Arkwright. Like its near neighbour upstream, Cressbrook Mill has until recently been badly neglected, but is currently under restoration.* (2)

(2) Orphaned apprentices enjoyed a better life at Cressbrook Mill. Despite working long hours, they were better fed and housed, and even given a rudimentary education which included Sunday walks on the nearby hillsides.

Watercress still grows in thickly-wooded Cressbrook Dale and wild peppermint can be found, its essence once distilled nearby. Terraced one-time millworkers' cottages in **Cressbrook** village seem to cling to the

Mysterious Peter's Stone in Cressbrook Dale.

Monsal Head Viaduct.

hillside above the mill and its castellated 'Apprentice House'. Walkers visiting Cressbrook can enjoy the rare privilege of eating their own sandwiches in 'Dave's Tea Stop' café. Handsomely built Victorian Cressbrook Hall, though privately owned, opens its gardens for special occasions.

'Dave's Tea Stop'
Cressbrook.

A narrow track climbs densely wooded **Cressbrook Dale**, another nature reserve, past the tiny group of houses of Ravensdale Cottages. Above them and to the east, is a cave where remains of prehistoric habitation were once found. The dale winds on, leaving behind its woodland, and at its head stands the enigmatic doleritic limestone outcrop known as Peter's Stone. Supposed to be the site of the last gibbet in Derbyshire, the tower is said to be haunted by the victim of this barbaric practice. He was hanged for the murder of a woman living in nearby Wardlow Mires, the cluster of houses and an old pub at the junction of the A623 Chesterfield road, and the B6465 Monsal Head road.

Well Dressing, a traditional Peakland custom.

Wardlow proper is a few yards higher along the B6465. Mostly roadside farmhouses, the village follows a line of springs, in a linear pattern unique to the Peak District. The village holds a flower festival and dresses its wells in early September.

Winding sinuously in a deep cutting within the limestone uplands, the main valley widens and is able to accommodate one or two small farms before the river makes one of its many sharp turns beneath **Monsal Head**. Here the the dale is crossed by its famously scenic viaduct, hated by Ruskin, and now part of the Monsal Trail. The roadside car park in front of the Monsal Head Hotel and above the viaduct is the place to enjoy what many consider to be one of the finest views in the Peak. Prehistoric man fortified the promontory of nearby Fin Cop. A walk between Monsal Head and Ashford in the Water passes beneath the airy vantage point on its way down Monsal Dale.

**Monsal Dale Walk
p158**

The twin Longstone villages sit comfortably along a minor road east from Monsal Head. **Little Longstone** is mostly stone cottages dating from the 16th and 17th centuries; its simple but welcoming pub, the Pack Horse was built about that time. **Great Longstone** as the name suggests, is the larger of the two villages. The privately owned brick-built hall, unusual in an area with a plentiful supply of building stone, dates from 1747. Stone cottages and larger houses fit around a small village green and of the pubs, the name of the Crispin has tenuous links with a local who, it is said, fought with King Henry V at the Battle of Agincourt.* Both Little and Great Longstone dress their wells annually.

Great Longstone and Little Longstone Well Dressings, late July

* Farming and lead mining, major local industries from medieval times until the last century, are commemorated by two interesting carvings in Great Longstone village church. One shows a milkmaid with a churn and the other a crouching miner. There is also a curious replica of the devil who seems to be climbing out of a tub, which with a little imagination could have him leaving a mine shaft.

Hassop is a couple of miles to the east of Great Longstone, and is dominated by the imposing Roman Catholic church built in 1818 for the Eyre family of nearby Hassop Hall. The 17th-century hall was enlarged in 1830 and is now an hotel and restaurant with an unusual wine cellar - it is part of a lead mine! Hassop once had a rather grand railway station, built not just to serve the village, but for the convenience of the Duke of Devonshire. The station yard is now a useful car park for the southern section of the Monsal Trail. An agricultural implement supplier and also a book retailer use the abandoned station buildings. There is also a small café where you can browse amongst the books on sale.

Countryside Bookstore Ltd, Hassop Station yard. Open 7 days a week.

The main road, the A6, rejoins the Wye at the bottom of steep Taddington Dale and there is a car park where you can stretch your legs and explore the surrounding part of the dale, hereabouts known as **Monsal Dale**. A footpath, through Great Shacklow Wood covering the

slopes south of the river, passes a sough draining Magpie Mine near Sheldon. Near this outpouring of water are two small and partly restored water powered mills where bobbins were made for local cotton mills. Trout destined to stock the nearby river are bred in the pool close to the point where the main road crosses the Wye.

Above and below: Traffic no longer uses Sheepwash Bridge, at Ashford in the Water.

Black marble, favoured by Victorians to decorate their churches, was quarried and polished at a water mill on the site of the council road depot, close to the point where a side road descends from Sheldon to join the A6 near the turning for **Ashford in the Water.** Originally built for packhorses, Sheepwash Bridge long closed to traffic, crosses the river from the main road and offers a scenic introduction to this attractive village. Sheep are no longer dipped in the pool below the bridge, but a convenient seat is a popular vantage point for photographers and local ducks on the look out for picnickers' crumbs.

The old market stand in Ashford in the Water.

* White paper garlands, or 'crants', still hang in Holy Trinity Church from the last time they were carried at the funeral of unmarried girls.

Ashford in the Water
Well dressings held in June.

Reaching Ashford's main street, the first thing of note by the bridge is the hexagonally roofed old market stand, then diagonally opposite and to its right is Holy Trinity Church.* Memorials carved from the locally quarried black marble adorn the church, several of them made around the mid-1700s by Samuel Watson of Heanor, who also used the stone to decorate the interior of Chatsworth. Although many of its houses date from the 18th century, a number were built in the 17th, including a tithe barn and its oldest inn, the Ashford, just one of a handful of places offering food to a very high standard.

A Shrove Tuesday curfew bell reminding Ashford housewives to make pancakes is no longer rung. Well dressing on the other hand is very much alive, with each of the five village wells dressed on the Saturday before Trinity Sunday, including one by the local primary school pupils. The local cricket team plays on the tree-shaded pitch across the Chesterfield road, creating the quintessential English country scene on fine summer evenings.

Below Ashford a weir holding back the river has created a pond that once powered mills in Bakewell. Backed by beech trees, it makes a perfect setting for the meadow path which can be followed on a riverside walk from Bakewell. Only Lumford Mill built by Arkwright in 1777 for cotton spinning and the first mill encountered on the approach to Bakewell, is still used for industrial purposes, with the others either made into flats or offices.

Two bridges span the Wye at Bakewell, the first a little downstream from Lumford Mill is a many-arched four foot wide packhorse bridge dating from 1664, built presumably to divert packhorse traffic around the busy town centre. Close to Holme Hall on the opposite side of the bridge, traces of an old mine can still be seen where chert, a flint-like stone used in pottery making, was mined until recently.

A path through Scot's Garden, a lovely stretch of water meadow, leads downstream to the venerable road bridge into **Bakewell** centre. Ducks and rainbow trout congregate below the bridge, the former hoping for crumbs from riverside picnickers. South of the bridge, can be seen the modern version of the market which has been held in the town since before the *Domesday* survey of 1086, and confirmed by charter in 1330. By 1826 the then street market was causing congestion and was moved behind the old market hall. Monday markets frequently create traffic problems, and in an attempt to ease the difficulty, are shortly to be transferred, as part of a controversial town centre redevelopment scheme, to a more modern site across the river.

Although there was once a wooden pallisaded castle above the river, the parish church on the hillside overlooking Bakewell is now the oldest recognisable building. Traces of its Saxon foundation can still be seen, together with stumps of two well preserved preaching crosses and ancient stone coffins in the porch. The inside of the church is well documented, especially the Vernon Chapel which has a fine memorial to Dorothy Vernon and her husband John Manners (see Haddon Hall).

A little way uphill by one of the typically narrow lanes, the **Old House Museum**, a well presented collection of local memorabilia, is housed in the early-Tudor house saved from demolition by the local historical society. Below the church, houses in Avenel Court date from around the same time, but are fronted by a Georgian

Ashford Lake Walk p 158

Bakewell Market
Cattle market, wide range of produce, clothing, household goods. Held every Monday.

Old House Museum
Bakewell, open daily throughout the summer.

shop exterior. The part-timbered Old Town Hall within the same group of buildings dates from 1684. It once housed almsmen on the ground floor, then when a row of almshouses was built to the rear of the building, for a time it became the local grammar school.

The Rutland Hotel overlooking the town square and war memorial was built by the Duke of Rutland around 1700 when he tried to establish Bakewell as a spa in competition with nearby Matlock and Buxton. Still fed by a natural spring, Bath House is in the top left hand corner of Bath Gardens. Unfortunately his scheme failed as the water was too cold for comfort.

As befits a market town, Bakewell is well served by inns and restaurants, there are even two pubs next door to each other in the market place, The Queen's Arms and The Peacock. Adjacent to them is the market hall now used as an exhibition and information centre by the Peak District National Park Authority. Shops of all types surround the market area, adding to the attractions of the town. Town wells are dressed at the time of Bakewell carnival, usually starting on the last Saturday in June, by craftsmen and women whose skills were displayed to the Queen Mother at the Chelsea Flower Show in 1977.

Top: Bakewell Pudding shop. Above: Horticulturists can show off their produce at Bakewell Show.

Bakewell Show
Held first week in August.

Bakewell Show is the high spot on the rural calendar of the Peak District. Held at the beginning of August, the show attracts competitors from far and wide, when pampered carefully groomed beasts are led round the show ring, or show jumpers take their place.

Haddon Hall.

Bakewell Well Dressings
late June.

A Norwegian princess competed in one year's show jumping event, but she was no match against local riders! Garden produce, floral displays, fly-casting instruction and Women's Institute stands, alongside commercial stalls, bungee jumping, helicopter rides, and the chance to meet friends and renew acquaintances, or possibly pick up a bargain, make the show the best event of the year.

Never, never, on pain of being thrown out of the shop, ask for a Bakewell Tart in Bakewell. **Bakewell Pudding** is the accurate description of this delicacy which is the town's culinary claim to fame. * Even though controversy surrounds who actually has the original recipe, one thing is sure, the popularity of Bakewell Puddings means they are exported all over the world.

Haddon Hall is hidden by trees from the A6 beyond Bakewell. Standing on a slight rise above the river, the medieval manor house is a unique example of building styles from the 12th to the 17th centuries. Abandoned in 1640 by its owners the Manners family, Earls then later Dukes of Rutland, when they moved to Belvoir Castle in Rutland, the building was never 'improved' by later fashions. The current state of the house is due to the father of the present Duke who in the early 1900s

* Several shops claim to hold the original recipe for Bakewell Pudding in their safes. Traditionally it was first made by the cook at the former White Horse Inn on Matlock Street, around 1860. Given instructions to bake a strawberry tart, the flustered cook mistakenly put the jam into the basin first, followed by egg and butter based flaky pastry mixture with a hint of almond essence. The result rather than being rejected, was an instant success and became a popular item on the inn's menu.

Haddon Hall is renowned for its rose garden.

Haddon Hall
Open daily, April to September.

* The medieval time capsule of Haddon Hall and its setting has been very popular with film makers. Part of ITV's Moll Flanders *was filmed here, as well as the BBC productions of the children's films,* The Chronicles of Narnia, *and* The Prince and the Pauper. *Franco Zeferelli used Haddon for* Lady Jane Grey, The Princess Bride *and* Jane Eyre *which also used other locations around the Peak District.*

decided to restore Haddon, devoting much of his life to the scrupulous work. The oldest part of the building is the chapel, followed by the impressive Long Gallery and banqueting hall with its minstrels' gallery, beneath which Sir John Manners, self styled king of the Peak, held long and boisterous Christmas celebrations.*****

The popular story of Dorothy Vernon's elopement with John Manners in 1563 tells of her crossing the terrace garden and meeting him by the narrow packhorse bridge below the hall. Unfortunately this is pure fiction as both garden and bridge along with the Dorothy Vernon steps down which she fled, were not built until at least 26 years later! Notwithstanding the facts of the matter, both bridge and garden are a delight, the latter having won awards in recent years.

The limestone Plateau

Villages scattered across the rolling green uplands of the **limestone plateau** are still mostly the homes of farm workers whose not so long ago ancestors made extra income from part-time lead mining. Apart from the

partly restored surface works of Magpie Mine, all that is left of this long dead industry are the humps and hollows that dot the surrounding landscape.

At the apex of a rough triangle made by the A6, A5012 and A515, **King Sterndale** is an almost hidden village. Sitting around a village green marked by an ancient stone cross beside the narrow road climbing high out of Ashwood Dale, King Sterndale's attraction lies in the magnificent views across the nearby dales. Its church inexplicably stands by itself about a mile to the south. Opposite the church a field path crosses **Deepdale** where a hoard of Roman coins and jewellery were found in the last century; you can see them in Buxton museum.

The path from Deepdale reaches **Chelmorton**, a single street of cottages and farms set back from a system of narrow fields away from any through road.* One of the highest villages in England, its narrow fields are still laid out as they were in medieval times, preserved by their well-maintained dry limestone boundary walls. The Church Inn stands at the end of the street and opposite is the 15th-century church of St John the Baptist. Wells are dressed around mid-June.

Chelmorton's preserved medieval field pattern.

Chelmorton and Deepdale Walk p 159

* Before piped water reached Chelmorton, householders relied upon a narrow stream known by the delightful name of Illy Willy Water.

On the high moor above Chelmorton, **Five Wells chambered burial cairn** where the remains of twelve skeletons were found, is a unique relic dating from neolithic times. The highest megalithic tomb in England, it can be visited by a concessionary footpath from the end of a field track (GR 123 711), close by Fivewells Farm.

Traffic mostly avoids **Taddington** as it speeds along the A6. The village street is a pleasant double line of stone cottages, farms, an inn and a few modern houses. Not content with front access, the rear of Taddington properties can also be reached by narrow paths parallel to the main street. The rather grand church was built on the profits of local wool and lead trades and was traditionally founded by Celtic missionaries in the seventh century, a link borne out by decorations on the venerable cross in the churchyard. Below the village, densely wooded Taddington Dale leads down to the River Wye, where in the valley bottom, traces of pre-historic habitation have been found.*

* Strip lynchets, a form of medieval terraced fields, can still be detected in fields around Priestcliffe across the A6 to the north of Taddington. They stand out best with the long shadows at sunset on summer evenings.

Flagg is another linear village, built along the line of its wells to the south of Taddington. The privately owned hall is Elizabethan and not open to the public, but it can be seen from the roadside near the village pub. **Flagg Point-to-Point Races** are held by the High Peak Hunt on Flagg Moor on Easter Tuesday.

Flagg Point-to-Point Races, Flagg Moor, A515. Trade stands, refreshments.

The name **Monyash** means 'Many Ashes' and from the plentiful supply of water in this normally dry upland, it is possible that there were a great number of ash trees growing hereabouts at one time. The village sits on a series of clay beds which were used since time immemorial to create 25 ponds, or 'meres', to give them their local name. Of these only Fere Mere, once used for drinking water, survives at the roadside behind the village primary school. Monyash once held a market, charter dating from 1340, on the small green marked by the ancient pillar of a stone cross outside the Bull's Head.

Magpie Mine $^1/_2$ mile south of Sheldon. Partially restored lead mine.

There was once a Barmote Court that met at Monyash to adjudicate mining disputes and settle claims. All that is now left of this industry are the partly restored surface remains of **Magpie Mine**, a little to the north of the Chelmorton to Bakewell road. Last worked in 1958, it dates from 1739 and is said to be haunted. Water still drains from the mineworkings through a man-made passage, or 'sough', and flows out into the

River Wye about 1³/₄ miles away to the north below Great Shacklow Wood. Preserved by the joint efforts of the Peak District Historical Society and the Peak District National Park Authority, the mine buildings together with examples of horse-operated winding systems, are an interesting reminder of an industry which once employed villagers from much of the surrounding countryside. Parking is on the roadside and plaques explain the various buildings and machinery on display.

On a side road on the heights above steep Kirk Dale close to the Magpie Mine, is the village of **Sheldon**. Once the home of lead miners, it is a rarely visited, single street of farms and 18th-century cottages set back from a double line of wide grass verges. Owing nothing to tourism and its attendant traffic, the pace of life in Sheldon is slow and all the better for that. The one pub, the Cock and Pullet has a small but varied menu, and is a welcome haven at times when the more popular parts of the Peak become crowded.

Top: High Peak Hunt, Flagg Races; (above) Monyash; (below) Magpie Mine near Sheldon.

The term 'Rake' is a Derbyshire word referring to small fault lines in the earth where lead and other minerals congregate.

Arbor Low Stone Circle, open all year.

Lathkill Dale river is an important trout stream.

Sitting on one of its highest points and with wide ranging views of the limestone plateau **Arbor Low** stone circle was built around 2,000 BC. Peakland's largest henge, it is classed as one of the most important neolithic monuments in Britain. Set within a 250ft diameter circular earth bank crossed by two causeways, 47 recumbent stones lie like the numbers on a giant clockface, with three central stones, which are also recumbent. Nearby about 350 yards to the south west, and reached by a short footpath, the tumulus of Gib Hill and an adjoining mound which marks the site of an earlier henge, complete the visible surface remains. The Roman road from *Lutudarum* (Carsington) to *Aquae Arnemetiae* (Buxton) is close by, following the line of a pre-historic trackway. Although there is no present day access, a ceremonial way linking this track to the henge, can still be traced along its approach through fields behind the present day plantation south west of Arbor Low. The henge is in the care of English Heritage and access to the site is from the car park adjacent to Arbor Low Farm (GR 158 637).

The road east from Arbor Low passes **Long Rake*** where fluorspa and other once waste products from old lead mines are processed. Although the fluorspa is worked out, the processing plant still functions and the line of the rake is marked by a shelter belt of trees along the roadside.

Lathkill Dale starts as a dry dale below Monyash village, with its stream emerging from a cave close to the narrowest section of the dale. To reach this point it is necessary to scramble over low boulders which have rolled down from long abandoned Ricklow Quarry above the dale's northern rim. Steps built by local conservation volunteers climb to fields surrounding the

quarry, and Parson Tor where a Monyash vicar fell to his death in 1776.

Mostly dry Cales Dale joins the Lathkill below **One Ash Grange Farm***(1). The wooded hillsides below the confluence of the two dales are now a nature reserve where such rarities as Jacob's Ladder (*polemonium caeruleum*) and Spurge Laurel (*daphne laureola*) grow.

(1) Granges were originally monastic farms and One Ash Grange was a penitentiary for misbehaving monks from Roche Abbey.

Just before the point where the path enters the wooded area at the foot of a small side dale from Haddon Grove, are the ruins of Carters' Mill. Once powered by a water wheel, the grindstones can still be seen part-buried by the side of an attractive weir. Stone pillars a little lower down the dale carried water to drive huge water wheels, the motive power required to pump water out of Lathkill Dale and Mandale lead mines. Of the two mines, Mandale's ruins are the best preserved. **Like all mine workings it is dangerous and it is advisable to view from a safe distance**.

The woodland path as far as Lathkill Lodge and the track to Over Haddon is privately owned, but walkers are allowed to use it on the understanding that the owners can still charge one penny on the Thursday of Easter week. **Over Haddon** sits on a terrace high above the dale and the Lathkill Hotel makes a good stopping place, and offers excellent food and drink. There is also a craft centre and tea rooms nearby.*(2)

* (2) In 1854 a gold mining venture close to Over Haddon saw shares reach £30 before the 'gold' was found to be iron pyrites, 'Fool's Gold', and the greedy speculators lost their money.

Deep pools downstream are stocked with trout and below Conksbury bridge, monster sized fish can often be seen lazing beneath the narrow pack horse bridge below Raper Lodge. Field paths continue downstream to **Alport** where the Lathkill is joined by the River Bradford. The quiet hamlet is a little way from the road, a pleasant group of stone cottages, a hump backed bridge and downstream, the remains of a mill where lead ore was prepared for smelting. Observant passers-by will see a curious notice on the gable of a farm on the Youlgreave road, warning vagrants to keep away.

Alport is where the Lathkill and Bradford Dales join.

**Youlgreave and
Lathkill Dale Walk
p 159**

**(1) Although the
Ordnance Survey and the
county council use the
first letter 'e' in the
'greave' part of
Youlgreave, the locals
spell the name Youlgrave,
but prefer to call it
'Pommy' just to confuse
visitors!*

**Youlgreave Well
Dressings
Late June.**

A walk following both Lathkill and Bradford Dale, starting at the Youlgreave roadside above Alport village, explores the unspoilt beauty of these two dales and the surrounding upland pastures.

High above the River Bradford, **Youlgreave***(1) one of the largest villages in the Peak manages to keep its rural atmosphere despite the pressures of modern living. The village proudly maintains its independent water supply brought by pipeline from beneath gritstone moorland to the south. Before this Youlgreave had a severe water problem, especially in dry summers when many of the village wells dried up. The circular stone tank opposite the one-time co-op shop, now a youth hostel, was used to store the piped water which first came to Youlgreave in 1829. Although the custom is quite possibly much older, the five village wells have been dressed since 1829 during the week following the Saturday nearest St John the Baptist Day.

Youlgreave has several buildings worth more than a passing glance, from farmhouses within the immediate confines of the village to its two-storied hall, the garden of which is often open during well dressing week. The church is a delight and contains the tombs of several medieval knights alongside its Norman font. Unusual in design, the font bowl is supported by a central column together with four small shafts. An upside down dragon on the main bowl holds a smaller bowl in its mouth, thought to have been made to hold consecrated oil. It has a curious history, having once stood in Elton church. The east window was designed by William Morris and Burne-Jones, the Pre-Raphaelite artists. Church records from 1609 to 1715 show fees paid to the official dog whipper.

Sleepy **Middleton-by-Youlgreave** sits above Bradford Dale, a group of farms and stone cottages with pretty gardens around a minor road junction.*****(2) The 19th-century archaeologist Thomas Bateman lived here at Lomberdale Hall. Together with teams of local labourers, he dug up numbers of ancient burial mounds, in a misguided search for treasure. A signpost at the side of the chapel points the way to his tomb surmounted by the replica of a Bronze Age urn.

**(2) During the Civil War
Christopher Fulwood
raised an army of 1,000
lead miners in support of
Charles I. Unfortunately
like his king, he was
unsuccessful and, after an
attack on his nearby
home, was killed while
hiding behind the rock
above Bradford Dale
which bears his name.*

Ponds with watercress growing on their margins line **Bradford Dale**. Once used to power Alport lead mill, they are now stocked with trout. Downstream and above a wide stone clapper bridge, the hillside café is a popular halt for walkers before they continue to explore the lower reaches of the dale, possibly watching climbers on German sounding Rhienstor.

Grassed over spoil heaps near Mawstone Farm on the slopes above Bradford Dale mark the site of Mawstone Mine. This is where the worst disaster in the history of Derbyshire lead mining occurred in the 1800s when firedamp, a form of methane, exploded, killing eight miners.

Two more villages must be included in this chapter before the Lathkill joins the Wye at Pickory Corner, once the site of a long abandoned village. High on the limestone moors, **Elton** is a cluster of north facing old houses where lead miners once delved beneath the surrounding land. They even disturbed the foundations of the church by (illegally) mining too close. The church font managed to find its way to Youlgreave and after years of wrangling, Elton had to make do with a replica.

Ancient remains are found in fields nearby to Elton. A mile north on Harthill Moor, Castle Ring (GR 221 628), is a prehistoric fort standing in a private field behind Harthill Moor Farm. Easily visible in another field close by, are four monoliths, the remains of a circle which once contained nine. The twin rock towers of Robin Hood's Stride once gave it the name, 'Mock Beggar Hall', from its similarity to a house when seen at dusk. Beneath Cratcliff Rocks on the opposite side of an ancient track beyond Robin Hood's Stride, is a hermit's cave decorated with a stone crucifix and a stone bench, the only form of comfort in the anchorite's cell. An easy stroll exploring the ancient remains, starts and finishes at Elton.

Elton and Robin Hood's Stride Walk p 159

The snug gritstone cottages of Stanton-in-Peak line a steep single roadway winding uphill from the B5056, to the northern limits of Stanton Moor, (see Chapter two). Narrow alleys lead into courtyards, giving the village an intimate atmosphere, only open to those who seek it out. Rare black fallow deer are owned by the Thornhills who have lived at Stanton Hall for generations and gave the village its church in 1839. The church's treasure is a water stoop dating from 1596, which was also donated by the Thornhills. Stanton has one inn, the 'Flying Childers', named after a racehorse belonging to the 4th Duke of Devonshire.

The Derwent Valley south of the Dark Peak

Rising in the wilderness of peat bogs and heather covered remote Bleaklow moors, the River Derwent undergoes many changes. Dammed in infancy, but once released, the river flows through some of the finest scenery in Derbyshire.

Chatsworth from the River Derwent.

North Lees, in Hathersage is a rare example of a fortified farmhouse.

Below Hathersage the banks of the Derwent are cloaked with natural woodland, a fitting introduction to the grandeur of Chatsworth. Beyond the park, the river scenery changes yet again, with water meadows on either side of Rowsley leading to the river's dramatic and sudden change of direction beneath the towering limestone crag of High Tor. Abrupt gritstone edges mark the eastern skyline, but the western slopes are gentler, denoting a change in the underlying rocks mainly to limestone.

Because of the marked change in character between the wilder northern section of the river and its more sylvan course downstream, this chapter deals with the Derwent Valley south from Hathersage, with the northern half described in the Dark Peak, chapter four.

Hathersage Open-Air Swimming Pool
Tel: 01433 640843 for opening times.

The best approach to **Hathersage** is by way of the A625 from Sheffield. Crossing Burbage Moor, the road suddenly rounds a bend at Surprise View, where the vista of Kinder Scout, Eyam Moor and the Derwent Valley is dramatically revealed. Hathersage sits in a sheltering curve of the valley bottom; a prosperous village, it has a good range of shops, including *Outside*, a well-stocked walking and climbing gear shop, together with hotels, restaurants and cafés to suit all needs; there is even an outdoor heated swimming pool.

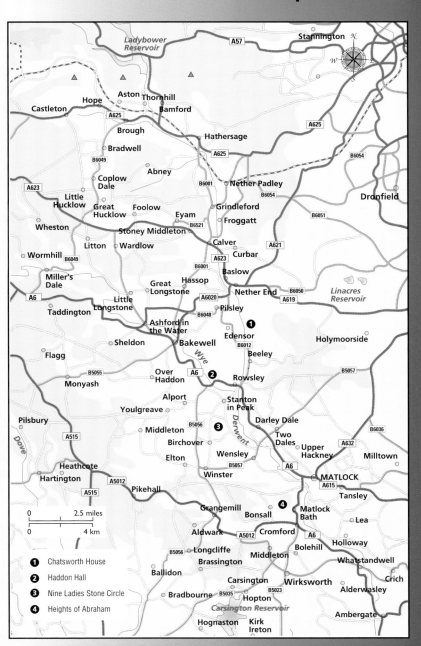

0   2.5 miles

0   4 km

❶   Chatsworth House
❷   Haddon Hall
❸   Nine Ladies Stone Circle
❹   Heights of Abraham

Little John's grave, Hathersage.

Carl Wark and Higger Tor Walk p 160

* There is much debate about the age of Carl Wark. Recent investigation suggests it dates from before the Iron Age, roughly 1000 years BC, but was refortified during the period of inter-tribal warfare following the Roman withdrawal from the Peak District.

Hathersage once had a needle, pin and wire drawing industry. No longer do the chimneys of its five mills 'belch out thick black smoke', as a 19th century visitor recorded, but the village retains its links with Sheffield industry in David Mellor's cutlery factory on the site of the old gas works. Built on the base of the gasometer, the award winning factory and its retail shop are sheltered by woodland beside the Grindleford road.

Little John, Robin Hood's lieutenant is, according to folk lore, buried in Hathersage churchyard. Two grave markers ten feet apart are supposed to be placed at his head and feet, and when the grave was opened in 1784, a 30 inch thigh bone was removed, suggesting it belonged to someone over eight feet tall! Unfortunately the bone subsequently disappeared, along with a huge longbow and green cap. Today the grave is cared for by the Ancient Order of Foresters.

Dedicated to St Michael, Hathersage church, though much altered in 1852, is built on ancient foundations and contains many interesting features such as the quaint gargoyles above the entrance porch. Monuments to members of the Eyre family adorn the interior, a family whose name inspired Charlotte Brontë to use the district in her romantic novel *Jane Eyre*. The Eyres were a powerful family and once owned seven manor houses around Hathersage, including North Lees, a fortified Elizabethan tower house, bought along with its farm and estate by the Peak District National Park in 1971.

At a time when the climate was milder, Celtic man built fortifications on the surrounding moors. Danish settlers are supposed to have built Camp Green on a tree covered hillock behind the church, but it is likely that it was there long before the Danes came. **Carl Wark** fort on Hathersage Moor can only be reached on foot from the Toad's Mouth Rock at the roadside below the remote moorland Fox House Inn. Arguably the most enigmatic fortification in the Peak, unlike other prehistoric forts which are mostly earth banked, Carl Wark's defences are made of stone. Massive boulders still give the impression of impregnability, together with the remains of hut circles and water troughs which have stood the test of time.***** Remnants of village settlements and stone circles on the nearby Lawrence Field moor indicate a large population lived on what is now rough moorland.

Higger Tor dominates the skyline above Carl Wark; its wild jumble of rocks though wall-like, are more natural than its lower neighbour. **Stanage Edge**, the rock climbers' playground runs north west in a high escarpment from the old road above Hathersage to Sheffield, before it peters out on Moscar Moor. A walk along its summit enjoys not only the views, but takes in several interesting features along the way. These range from a series of shallow troughs, carved and numbered by gamekeepers to collect drinking water for the grouse population on the moor, to an ancient flagged packhorse-way which joined the Long Causeway Roman Road at Stanage Edge. The tall waymark pole about half a mile further along the moor, has guided travellers for centuries, and finally Robin Hood's Cave, a draughty, almost inaccessible hollow in the cliff face, could certainly have offered refuge to bandits in the past.

**Stanage Edge Walk
p 160**

National Trust's **Longshaw Estate** covers much of the surrounding moors. The old shooting lodge is converted into flats and is not open, but there is a visitor centre and shop in part of the outbuildings. Guided walks take place on advertised days, or may be booked by groups. The famous **Longshaw Sheepdog Trials** take place in early September.

Longshaw Sheepdog Trials and other events Tel: 01433 651852 for details.

Abandoned grindstones lie around the rocks and old quarries of the eastern edges. Once in great demand by industries ranging from flour milling to wood pulp making and metal grinding, Derbyshire millstones were considered to be the finest available. Plant modernisation, not the least being the switch from stone to steel rollers by the Scandinavian wood pulp makers, spelt the death-knell for this not-so-ancient industry.*****

Grindleford Station at the mouth of Totley Tunnel, still the longest land based railway tunnel in Britain outside the London Underground system, is an ideal starting point to explore the confines of **Padley Gorge**. Protected from sheep grazing by its steep and rocky nature, it is one of the few relics of natural oak woodland. The old station café does not go in for *haute cuisine*, but offers such delights as all-day breakfasts of monumental proportions, served with pint-sized mugs of tea and coffee, ideal food for hardy outdoor types!

* Visitors are often puzzled by the vast numbers of millstones lying around the woods and bracken slopes below the edges. Quarrymen made them in their spare time, usually in winter, awaiting orders which mostly came in summer, a busy time for quarrying. The millstones are simply the result of anticipating a demand which never came.

Nether and **Upper Padley** villages are mostly residential, but the latter was once the scene of a

A pilgrimage is made each July to Padley Chapel.

terrible example of religious intolerance. In Elizabethan times a substantially built hall owned by the Catholic Fitzherbert family, stood on the flat valley bottom. In 1588 two priests Nicholas Garlick and Robert Ludlam were arrested and for practising their faith, were hanged, drawn and quartered at Derby. Thomas Fitzherbert died in the Tower of London in 1591, and his brother at Fleet Prison in 1598. Although the house was sold in 1657, it was eventually abandoned and fell into ruin. In 1933 the Nottingham Roman Catholic Diocese bought the property and restored **Padley Chapel**, to which a pilgrimage is made each July. Brunts Barn owned by the Peak National Park is opposite and nearby is an award winning wildflower nursery.

* Stoke Hall was once the home of William Cavendish whose support of King Charles I cost him the equivalent of a million pounds in today's terms. He would have made an excellent example of a Hollywood cavalier, and one can imagine him haughtily smoking his pipe before joining the fray at the Battle of Marston Moor.

Froggatt is a secluded group of gritstone houses fronted by pretty gardens beneath the wooded slopes of its namesake edge. A two-arched bridge dating from the 17th century spans the river and the road leads to Stoke Hall, now an hotel.* A statue called *Fair Flora* which once adorned Stoke Hall is now in Stoke Woods near the caravan park. Who Fair Flora was is open to debate, but the statue is certainly a delightful addition to the woodland scene.

A three-arched bridge controlled by traffic lights leads the Sheffield road into **Grindleford**. Above the village

Sir William Hill is named after Sir William Saville, second Marquis of Halifax, Lord of the Manor of Eyam in the late 17th century. Part of an ancient saltway from Cheshire, the road climbs steeply on to Eyam Moor.

Almost five hundred years old, the Barrel Inn at **Bretton** on Eyam Edge is a friendly pub catering for those who seek refreshment in tranquil surroundings. The views south from the 1,200 ft vantage point beggar description, making the Barrel an ideal stopping place on a hot summer's day, or at any other time for that matter. About 1$\frac{1}{2}$ miles to the north west is Camphill where members of the **Gliding Club** take to the air. Ever on the lookout for new members, the club has open days throughout the year.

During the lifetime of the writer and broadcaster L. du Garde Peach, **Great Hucklow** supported a live theatre from 1921 to 1971 which drew audiences from far beyond local villages. Little remains of the efforts of the long dead miners who dug lead from beneath surrounding fields, but fluorspa is now extracted from a modern mine at the head of nearby Bradwell Dale.

Foolow has a village green, a rarity in the Peak District, with a village cross, pond and bull-ring at its centre. The name Foolow is not a comment on the

Ducks wait for handouts near Foolow village pond.

Derbyshire and Lancashire Gliding Club
Trial flights available.

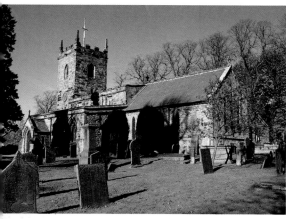

Eyam Church.

Eyam Well Dressings
Held at the end of
August/early September.

Eyam Church
Many interesting
features.

** Boulders cut with small
holes where money,
soaked in vinegar to act
as a disinfectant, could be
left as payment for
essential goods, still mark
the parish boundary.
These were the only link
with the outside world.
Several can still be seen,
for example next to the
path between Stoney
Middleton and the
Lydgate end of Eyam, or
beside Mompesson's Well
on the Bretton road above
the village.*

sensibilities of the villagers, but should be spelt Foo's Low, in memory of some long dead Saxon named Foo who first settled by the small nearby hill, or 'low'.

Much has been written about the brave stand **Eyam** made against the plague in 1665 and 1666. Although there has recently been a suggestion that rather than bubonic plague, the village suffered an outbreak of measles, most authorities will stick to the traditional story. Apparently the bacterium was carried to the village by fleas in a box of cloth sent from London to a tailor, George Viccars who was lodging with the Widow Cooper in one of the cottages by the church. On 7 September 1665, the first deaths were recorded. William Mompesson and his puritan predecessor Thomas Stanley united to hold the village together and persuaded the inhabitants to isolate themselves from the rest of the world. This brave decision prevented the plague from spreading, but not before a large part of the population had died, including Mompesson's young wife Katherine. She died on 25 August 1666, tragically one of the last. Her tomb stands in the churchyard next to the Celtic Cross, but few others were as fortunate in their last resting place. Mompesson sensibly closed the church in order to keep people apart, but held outdoor services in **Cucklet Dell** a small limestone dale opposite Eyam Hall. Families had to bury their dead where they could, in graves now marked by poignant memorials which still dot the surrounding fields. In all 259 people died from a total of 76 families.* The annual service held in Cucklet Dell on the last Sunday in August, remembers those who died in the plague.

Present day Eyam, incidentally the locals pronounce it E'em, is still laid out in the pattern of houses which would be instantly recognised by the Jacobean minister William Mompesson. Although many of its inhabitants rely upon the nearby quarries for their employment, the village sits aloof, high above the noise and dust of quarries across Middleton Dale. The church, the focal point of the village, has several interesting links with village history, from a cupboard reputed to be made of wood from George Viccar's fateful box which brought the plague to Eyam, to Mompesson's register of those terrible days, and his chair, rescued from a junk shop. The most wonderful sight in this church is the series of 16th-century wall paintings rediscovered as recently as 1963. Outside stand some medieval grave slabs, **Katherine Mompesson's grave** and an 18th-century sundial and the finest Celtic cross in Derbyshire – once a wayside cross standing to the west of the village at Cross Low. In the modern section of the graveyard is the amusing epitaph to Harry Bagshaw the Derbyshire and MCC cricketer who died in 1927. His gravestone with its cricketing symbols is not hard to find and is well worth the search.

Eyam Hall, home of the Wright family since 1676, sits back from the main street behind a walled garden entered through a fine wrought iron gateway. A fine example of a Jacobean Derbyshire manor house, it is open to visitors who can enjoy its impressive stone flagged floors, tapestry room and bedroom complete with its magnificent tester bed. Special events throughout the year range from outdoor concerts and plays to Christmas when the house is decorated in festive Victorian style.

Eyam's Celtic preaching cross once stood on Cross Low to the west of the village.

Eyam Hall
17th-century manor house, craft centre, buttery and gift shop.

Eyam Hall and the ancient village stocks.

Eyam Museum
Open March to
November.

**Eyam and Black Harry
Walk p 160**

The village also has a small but well presented museum opposite the main car park. Here the story of the plague is traced in graphic detail, together with features of Eyam geology.

Limestone quarries above Middleton Dale provide aggregate for road building. A path climbing above Darlton Quarry can be used as a vantage point to view at a safe distance, the complex beds of limestone made visible by the quarry workings. Beyond the quarry the path leads past a mound, the site of an abandoned limekiln, where an interpretive plaque brings it to life.

Fluorspa gathered from old lead workings throughout the Peak is processed at Laporte's Cavendish Mill but long ago this is where the notorious highwayman Black Harry plied his trade. From Black Harry Gate south of Cavendish Mill, a track below Longstone Edge leads down Coombes Dale, past Sallet Hole Mine, a lead mine where fluorspa was later worked, to the outskirts of **Stoney Middleton.** High limestone cliffs, once blackened by the smoke of 18th-century kilns, are now the province of rock climbers who can start many of their routes almost at road level.* Most of the older part of the village is hidden from the busy main road. Many of the roadside houses date from around 1840, when the turnpike trustees laid out what is still called New Road. An octagonal tollhouse from that time is now a chip shop, probably the only listed chip shop in the Peak District.

In 1762 Hannah Baddeley, jilted by her lover, tried to end it all by jumping off one of these cliffs. Luckily her voluminous petticoats acted like a parachute and she landed safely in a bush with little more hurt than her dignity!

Stoney Middleton church dates from 1415 when Joan Eyre endowed it in thanks for the safe return of her husband after the Battle of Agincourt. The present church is also octagonal in design, built around 1759 with a unique lantern tower. Close by the church the restored bath house, where the waters flow at a constant 21° C (70° F), is thought to have once been Roman. The village dresses three wells around the fourth Saturday in July, a custom which began in 1936.

**Stoney Middleton Well
Dressings**
Held at end of July.

East and west of the river the twin villages of **Calver** and **Curbar** mark the transition between the rugged grandeur of the upper reaches of the Derwent and the pastoral meadows leading to Chatsworth. Today the villages provide homes for Sheffield commuters as well as quarry workers from nearby Middleton Dale. **Calver**

Mill, once powered by two 22ft diameter waterwheels, dates from 1786, but instead of cotton, it now makes stainless steel sink units. The TV series *Colditz*, used the mill as its version of the WW2 prison camp. A more genuine 'prison' can be found in Curbar, where the conical-roofed village lock-up once held convicts overnight on their way to Chesterfield.

Boot and shoe making was once an important industry around Calver Sough and you can still pick up a bargain at the shoe factory shop beyond the traffic lights. Along with a petrol station, restaurant, pub, garden centre and a beautifully laid out alpine nursery, the area around Calver Sough* offers reason enough for stopping.

Fir Croft Alpine Nursery, in Calver Sough.

* The word 'sough' in Calver Sough indicates the proximity of a drainage channel carrying water from lead mines beneath limestone hills around Longstone Edge. Many of these channels were of considerable length and were built at great expense in the heyday of lead mining.

A little way along the road and in Calver village itself is the craft centre where you can enjoy home made food as an alternative to browsing in the shop. Diagonally opposite are the premises of a high class bespoke village tailor; and a little way along the road towards Baslow is Cliff College Methodist Conference Centre, where summer tented events attract visitors from all over the world.

The gritstone edges continue their march along the eastern lip of the Derwent Valley and the view from **Curbar Edge** is considered one of the finest. The view from the National Trust car park at **Curbar Gap** takes in the rolling hills beyond Eyam Moor to the right, and then leftwards along the wooded valley beyond Baslow are the rolling parklands of Chatsworth.

Packhorses once wound their way through a natural break in the gritstone escarpment. Level walking along the edges on either side of the gap can also be linked to a path around Big Moor where the remains of pre-historic hut circles and cairns tell of a once different population and their lifestyle. **Lady's Cross** (GR 273 783), a little to the south of the path from the Grouse Inn and the B6054 road between Owler Bar and the Fox

Curbar and Froggatt Edges Walk p 161

House Inn, once a marker for travellers across the moor, stands near an ancient earth bank, probably a tribal boundary when people lived on Big Moor.

The escarpment edge continues south above the Derwent.* A rough track climbing from Baslow to Bar Brook predates the modern and lower road and was built as the turnpike linking Sheffield and Bakewell. The prominent pillar high above the wooded Bar Brook ravine was erected in 1866 commemorating Wellington's victory at the Battle of Waterloo. **Gardom's Edge** towers above the opposite skyline of Bar Brook. **Birchen Edge** is a second tier set back from the main escarpment and here another pillar commemorates Admiral Horatio Nelson. Three natural rocks behind the edge are, with a little imagination, like the prows of men-of-war, carved with the names of three of Nelson's ships of the line at Trafalgar; *Victory, Defiance* and *Soverin* (sic).

Recent excavations on the rough moor between Gardom's and Birchen Edges, have led to the understanding of much of the complex and sophisticated lifestyle of the people who occupied this area several thousand years ago. One of the most interesting finds was a boulder beautifully carved with a series of 'cup and ring' marks. Visitors are welcome to visit the excavations throughout the summer, when conducted tours are arranged. The best approach is from the car park next to the Robin Hood Inn at the side of the A619 Chesterfield road from Baslow. A visit to the site can be included with a walk along Birchen Edge.

Baslow stands at the junction of the A619 Bakewell to Chesterfield road and the A623 Manchester road, at the northern end of Chatsworth Park. The old road into the village crosses a lofty three-arched bridge still with its little stone-built toll house. Baslow's church stands on even older foundations than its 19th-century appearance suggests. Saxon coffin stones are built into the church lintels, and knotwork thought to be from a stone cross of that time can be seen in and around the porch. The low tower and spire are at least 700 years old, with its clock with the words and letters VICTORIA 1897, commemorating the queen's jubilee, in place of numerals. Near the door is a whip once used for driving dogs out of the church.

Stone-gabled Bubnell Hall across the river is privately owned. The present hall was built in the 17th century

* On Baslow Edge the detached moorland rock known as the Aigle or Eagle Stone, said to turn at cockcrow, was once a test of manhood for young men living in nearby villages. They had to climb the rock before they were allowed to marry.

Gardom's Edge
Excavation of Bronze Age site. For details, Tel: 01629 816200

Birchen Edge Walk
p 161

on the site of a homestead belonging to the Basset family, one of whose ancestors signed the Magna Carta, and another who went to the Crusades with Richard the Lionheart.

Despite its smallness, Baslow is really five inter-linked hamlets, Bubnell, Bridge End, Over End, Nether End and Far End. Most of the village is around the church where there is a handful of village-type shops, a couple of pubs and Fisher's Restaurant at Baslow Hall. More shops including a high class dress shop, together with two more road side pubs and cafés are set around a tiny village green at Far End. Overlooking them all is the Cavendish Hotel, part of the Chatsworth Estate and popular with visiting foreign businessmen. Set back from the Chesterfield road beyond the village, the impressive Golden Gates mark the formal entrance to Chatsworth Park. They are used by Her Majesty the Queen on her visits to the house.

Renowned as one of the Seven Wonders of the Peak, **Chatsworth House,** the seat of the Dukes of Devonshire, ranks in architectural merit with the finest of all British great houses. The original hall which held the captive Mary Queen of Scots was a tudor manor, built on the site of an even older dwelling by the Countess of Shrewsbury, better known as Bess of Hardwick. All that is left of that house is the raised walled garden where the

Chatsworth, house and garden.

Stand Tower, Chatsworth's Elizabethan Hunting Tower.

Top: Chatsworth from the park.
Above: Fox hounds at Chatsworth Game Fair.

imprisoned queen took her ease, and the hunting tower overlooking the house from Stand Wood. The tudor walled garden, Queen Mary's Bower, is to the left of the roadway on approaching the house by way of the Edensor bridge. This bridge built in 1760, is reputed to be haunted by the ghost of a young servant girl, jilted by her lover.

The house we see today dates mostly from the late 17th century when the 4th Earl who later became the 1st Duke of Devonshire, with the Dutch architect William Talman, tried to alter Bess's Tudor mansion in the Classical style, but found it impossible to combine the two designs. Starting all over again, and with the help of another architect Thomas Archer, a contemporary of Sir Christopher Wren, the earl built the magnificent Palladian mansion overlooking the Derwent. The last major changes to the house were made in 1820 by the 6th Duke of Devonshire, the 'Bachelor' Duke, when the north or Theatre Wing was added, to the designs of Sir Jeffry Wyatville. The 6th Duke also altered the great Painted Hall and other formal apartments, and decorated them with the works of great masters such as Rembrandt, Van Dyck, Sir Joshua Reynolds and many other artists. Delicately lifelike wood carvings by Grinling Gibbons and Samuel Watson from nearby Heanor are there to be admired.*(1)

Anyone who has had to lay out a garden should spare a thought for the 6th Duke and Sir Joseph Paxton who designed Chatsworth's splendid gardens. Here is horticulture on the grand scale. Boulders brought from the surrounding edges are stacked one upon the other to create a Cyclopean rock garden. Fountains and cascades tumble down the hillside; the Emperor Fountain which can send a jet 290 feet into the air, was built to impress a visiting Czar of Russia, who unfortunately failed to arrive. Water to power the Emperor comes from a series of man-made lakes in Stand Wood high above the house. Recently installed turbines to generate electricity for the hall, are powered from the same source.*(2) The orangery where exotics such as bananas grow, and a maze, formal rose gardens, the Golden Garden commemorating the present Duke and Duchess's Golden Wedding, together with a humorous 'Cottage Garden' complete the exterior floral gardens. A unique recent addition is the raised vegetable garden. Most of the lower part of the formal garden is accessible to the disabled.

A **children's adventure playground and a farmyard** full of friendly animals and a reasonably priced

(1) Of all the wonders on show at Chatsworth a single item stands out in more than one sense. This is the painting of a fiddle on the back of the music room door, which came complete with the door, from the Devonshire residence in Piccadilly, London. It is so lifelike that attempts have been made to lift it down from the door on more than one occasion.

(2) The Willow Fountain, a lifelike metal tree, often catches the unwary, and is just one of the scores of ornamental additions to the gardens of Chatsworth.

Chatsworth House
House, extensive gardens, restaurant, gift shops. Open every day March to November.

Chatsworth Farmhouse and Adventure Playground
Range of farm animals, daily milking demonstration. Open Easter to end of September.

Chatsworth Garden Centre
Restaurant, open all year.

restaurant complete the amenities of the house. There is also a small restaurant attached to the **Chatsworth Garden Centre** by Calton Lees hamlet at the southern end of the park. Russian Cottage is in New Piece Wood above Calton Lees, which together with Swiss Cottage beyond Stand Wood was built as a romantic folly in Victorian times. As both houses are private, there is no access to either.

Paxton built a Great Conservatory at Chatsworth, which has since been demolished, but it served as a model for his Crystal Palace at the Great Exhibition of 1851. While at Chatsworth he became friends with George Stephenson, the railway and locomotive engineer who was living in retirement at Chesterfield. The two had a bet as to who could grow the straightest cucumber, a feat lately demanded by European Community bureaucrats. The engineer won by growing his cucumbers in specially made glass tubes!

The glorious parkland of Chatsworth was originally designed by 'Capability Brown' in 1760, and the best way to enjoy the finest view of the house is by taking the walk which follows the riverbank opposite the house, passing along the way the ruins of a water-powered corn mill. Leaving the park, the walk crosses a narrow hump-backed bridge in order to reach the estate village of Beeley. Here the path climbs through Hell Bank Plantation where the climbing ends. Half a mile to the north, on the edge of Gibbet Moor is **Hob Hurst's House**, an ancient tumulus said to be haunted by a hobgoblin.* The walk crosses open hillside and then returns to Chatsworth by way of Stand Wood and the Tudor Hunting Tower. This is a walk for all seasons, but perhaps late July is the best time when the scented heather is in bloom, covering the moors with a rich purple stretching almost to the distant horizon.

**Chatsworth Walk
p 161**

* Heather-clad Gibbet Moor is where a murderer was hanged, alive and in chains, then left to starve to death. His screams were so terrible that the then Duke took steps to end this barbaric punishment.

As well as work on the formal gardens, Paxton was also responsible for the major upheaval that befell the inhabitants of **Edensor**. In his day, the village overlooked Chatsworth House, which both he and the 6th Duke decided rather spoilt the view. Rather than try to screen it with trees, practically the whole village was moved lock stock and barrel to its present site. An architect provided the Duke with a catalogue of house designs, expecting him to choose one or two to be used for the whole village. However, the Duke was so impressed that he decided to have one of each design and as a result, Edensor, it is pronounced 'Ensor', is a village where no two houses are to the same design. Only one house of old Edensor remains, this is the cottage which stands in a walled garden on the opposite side of the road from the new village, and whose tenant refused to move. Fortunately the cottage could not be seen from Chatsworth House, and so the Duke allowed it to remain. Since then the cottage has been known as *Naboth's Vineyard* from the biblical character who defied a king.

The tall slender spire of St Peter's Church in Edensor, beckons across the park and is the estate church for Chatsworth. This is where Her Majesty the Queen worships when she visits Chatsworth, and also where the Sheep Service of Thanksgiving is held every spring. Built in 1867 to Sir Gilbert Scott's design in the early English style, it contains many features taken from an earlier church which had stood on the site for centuries. Here are memorials ranging from the simple brass plate to John Beton, Mary Queen of Scot's servant who died while serving his queen at Chatsworth, to a huge and costly memorial in the Cavendish Chapel to the memory of two of Bess of Hardwick's sons, and to William Ist Earl of Devonshire who helped James I colonise Bermuda.*

* Of all the memorials at Edensor Church it is a simple grave that draws most attention, especially from visiting Americans. This is the grave of Kathleen Kennedy, sister of the late President John F Kennedy, who was killed in an air crash. She was the widow of the present Duke's eldest brother, the Marquis of Hartington who died on active service in World War 2.

Hidden in a fold of the hills and overlooking the Derwent Valley, **Pilsley** is another estate village. Its houses are much older than those in Edensor, and create a typically English village scene. There is one pub, but perhaps the biggest attraction is the **Chatsworth Farm Shop** built into converted stud stables above the village. This is where high quality produce from the Chatsworth Estate is sold, ranging from freshly baked loaves, to prime beef and game reared or caught on the estate.

Chatsworth Farm Shop
Open all year selling produce from the Estate.

Beeley is the final estate village surrounding Chatsworth Park. Set back from the road behind its pretty church where wild daffodils bloom in spring, Beeley was laid out by Joseph Paxton for the 6th Duke, but contains many older houses. The Devonshire Arms offers good food in an early 17th-century setting.

At **Rowsley**, the Derwent is joined by the River Wye, the junction of two famous trout streams. For many years Rowsley was the northern terminus of the Midland Railway, but all that is left is the station house designed by Paxton that stands below the corner of the A6 and Beeley roads. It was due to the stubborn refusal of the Duke of Devonshire that the railway never followed its planned route through Chatsworth Park. Peak Rail, the society devoted to restoring the line hope that one day trains will again run along the line that both the Duke of Devonshire and his neighbour the Duke of Rutland allowed as a compromise.

Rowsley is in two halves, one part being the one-time railway houses on the Beeley road, and the other, much older part set back from the main road on the other side of the river. An estate village for nearby Haddon with many of its houses over 300 years old, it has two well known hostelries, the Peacock and the Grouse and Claret. Of these the former is the older and dates from 1652, but both are popular with visiting anglers. The nearby Grouse and Claret, originally the station hotel, takes its name from the game bird and a trout fly. Down a side road opposite the Peacock, **Caudwell's Mill** still grinds wholemeal flour by traditional methods, though not on a commercial basis and provides visitors with an insight into flour milling.

Caudwell's Mill
Working flour mill and craft workshops. Open to visitors.

Darley Dale astride the A6, was once home for railway workers from the Northwood Sidings near Rowsley. Now completely overgrown, the sidings have become something of an unofficial nature reserve where wild orchids grow alongside the rare Herb Paris.* **Two Dales**, almost part of Darley Dale, fits snugly into the valley bottom of its twin deeply wooded dales, Hall and Sydnope. Both are semi-natural, the former being owned by the Woodland Trust,and the latter enhanced by a series of old mill ponds once feeders for a flour mill at their foot. The mill is no longer powered by water, but still operates, making cattle and other animal feeds. Sydnope Hall set in secluded woodland above the dale head, is converted into privately owned flats and has a garden reputed to be built by Paxton .

Sir Joseph Whitworth, the Manchester engineer lived at Stancliffe Hall, Darley Dale, which is now a private school. He gave the Whitworth Institute to the village, along with an hotel and a hospital, intending them to be the nucleus of a much larger village, that never developed.

Horses in fields beside the A6 close by the DFS furniture warehouse, are owned by the **Red House Stables**, a working carriage museum and driving school offering training from novices up to the skills required for driving four-in-hands. The well preserved vehicles,

Red House Stables Carriage Museum
Over 40 horse-drawn vehicles. Open all year.

including a stage coach and royal mail coach, are regularly seen on local roads and many have featured in films and TV series.

The medieval parish church of St Helen is closer to the river, away from the main part of Darley Dale, part of the hamlet of Churchtown. Well worth a visit, it contains many interesting features, some of them dating from Roman and Saxon times.*

A side road by the Whitworth Hotel leads past the operational headquarters of **Peak Rail** and its collection of rolling stock, to the Square and Compass inn and 15th-century Darley Bridge. Crossing the bridge the road turns sharply to the right then left, to pass through the village, where a side road on the right leads upwards towards the mysterious rocks and heather of Stanton Moor. Before the road makes its final and steeply swinging climb to the moor, it passes the site of Mill Close Mine, Derbyshire's last and most productive lead mine. Abandoned in 1938, the main site is now used by a metal reclamation factory, but some of the earlier subsidiary workings can be seen nearby, especially in Clough Wood.

Above: Red House Stables, Darley Dale. Interested bystanders, Peak Rail (below).

*A famous yew tree stands in St Helen's churchyard, close to the porch. Reputed to be well over a thousand years old, the evergreen branches stem from a trunk over 32 feet round.

Peak Rail
Regular steam trips from Matlock to Rowsley. Tel: 01629 580381 for details.

Nine Ladies Stone Circle, Stanton Moor.

Stanton Moor Walk p 162

* A lone tower on Stanton Moor erected in 1832 on the eastern escarpment overlooking the valley, is dedicated to Earl Grey, not for inventing the well known blend of tea, but for steering the Reform Act through Parliament. This was the act which began the move towards universal voting rights.

Tiny hillside hamlets guard the way to **Stanton Moor**. A gritstone outlier set amidst miles of limestone, the 1,096ft high moor was once greatly revered by our prehistoric ancestors who littered the moor with cairns and stone circles. A level footpath winding its way around the moor, passes many of these features, such as the **Nine Ladies Stone Circle**, and their attendant 'King', who are said to be dancers turned to stone for dancing on the Sabbath.* Another feature, the Cork Stone, so named from its similarity to a champagne cork, with iron rungs set into its face, tempts the adventurous to scale its heights. Although the rungs were placed there by quarrymen in the 1800s, it is possible the stone, which has a deeply carved basin on its summit, had some ancient religious purpose.

Finely grained gritstone used for building purposes is quarried on the edges of Stanton Moor with many of the workers living in nearby **Birchover**. Houses built over a period of 300 years fit higgledy-piggledy around the single main street.The village has two inns, the Red Lion where a 30ft well inside the main bar is capped by a thick clear glass cover, and the Druid Inn, famed for its food. The latter was named after druids who, if folklore is correct, once practised their magic amidst **Rowtor Rocks** immediately above the inn. Once it was felt necessary to hire guides to reach the summit of this

strange group of boulders, but providing care is exercised, the rocks can safely be explored in half an hour or so.*

A little-used road south from Birchover passes the scattering of farms and cottages of Upper Town, where in front of one of them is a well preserved set of village stocks. The road continues southwards for a little over a mile, across the head of a secluded valley to **Winster**. The village was already old in the 17th and 18th centuries when many of its houses were built. Half hidden at the end of narrow 'jitties', or 'ginnels', depending on who is giving directions, but alleyways to the rest of us, the cottages sprang up in the hey-day of lead mining, for this was one of the most prosperous mining villages in the Peak. All around are the humps and hollows, and stone beehive caps of long abandoned mines. The double-gabled dower house at the end of the street leading towards the half hidden church, is the largest private house in the village, but pride of place must surely be given to the **Market House**. Dating from the 16th and 17th centuries its once open-arched ground floor was filled in to shelter traders. The upper floor, built in the 17th century, unusually for this area in brick, completes the sturdy and once busy centre of village life. Owned by the National Trust, it became their first Derbyshire property in 1906.

The Druid Inn, Birchover's popular eating place.

* *The fairly steep but short climb of Rowtor Rocks is worth the effort, if only to admire the view, but the summit rocks have a surprise in store. Seats, rooms and steps lead off in all directions, the work of an eccentric 18th-century clergyman, the Reverend Thomas Eyre, who entertained his friends and composed sermons on this high vantage point.*

Winster Market House
National Trust
Information Centre, open
April to October.

Winster Market House.

Winster has a thriving community, where a hotly contested pancake race is held in the main street following the ringing of the Shrove Tuesday bell. Wakes Week festivities take place at the end of June when the renowned Winster Morris Men can usually be seen dancing, and there is a village market on summer Bank Holiday weekends. Around Christmastide, guisers go from house to house and to pubs in the area, dressed in strange costumes to perform a play which probably started in the 18th century. Beer was once thought to cure lead poisoning, a constant problem to the miners, and at one time there were over twenty inns in Winster. Nowadays the village has only two, but excellent pubs, the Bowling Green in the centre of Winster, and the Miners' Standard on its outskirts. The standard referred to in the pub's name, was a dish used to measure lead ore, and above the inn, an open fronted building beside the B5056 Grangemill road was used to store the ore prior to smelting.

Moving back towards the Derwent valley, the road drops down through **Wensley Dale**, not the Yorkshire dale, but a short, pretty, dry dale where the Red Lion in Wensley village seems to be only opened at the whim of the landlord! A walk from Winster explores Wensley Dale and also the limestone uplands surrounding Winster.

**Winster Walk
p 162**

Just before the road enters Darley Bridge, a side turning leads past Oker Hill, or to use its local name, One Tree Hill. Lonely Will Shore's tree stands exposed on top of the little hill, strangely unbent by the wind. Folk tales surround it with magic properties, but the most romantic tells us it is the survivor of two planted by the Shore brothers on their final parting.

Passing the studio where Pollyanna Pickering, the internationally renowned wildlife artist, holds exhibitions from time to time, the road winds through **Snitterton.** Here the partly overgrown bull ring, a moat and medieval

field terraces, hint of a once larger and older village. The privately owned hall is a fine example of a small Elizabethan two-storied house, built to the then traditional 'E' plan in tribute to the Tudor queen. Nearby Snitterton Manor Farm also dates from the 16th century.

A relaxing afternoon fishing in Lumsdale.

Heading to the **Matlocks** from Snitterton the road skirts abandoned limestone quarries where, if current plans come to fruition, there will soon be a large supermarket and sports amenities.

Bentley Brook once powered mills in narrow Lumsdale.

The name Matlock is attached to several areas of habitation in this tight corner of the Derwent valley. Matlock proper has seen its centre move radically from place to place, especially within the last century. Originally Matlock Green was the focal point, where a fortnightly cattle market was held in the roadway below the ancient church. Early industry took hold nearby in steep and narrow **Lumsdale**, which can be reached by a narrow side road to the left of the Alfreton road. Here the Bentley Brook tumbling through a narrow wooded ravine powered a series of mills, and where today a short walkway winds between the ruins of mills preserved by the locally based Arkwright Society. Explanatory plaques erected by the society help

bring back to life the bustle of industry in this forgotten corner.

Matlock's heyday was in the 19th century when the eccentric industrialist John Smedley built the massive hydro that stands high above the town, and is now the headquarters of Derbyshire County Council. So popular was Smedley's theory of the use of water to cure most ills, better known as hydropathy, that thousands, among them the rich and famous, flocked to Matlock in order to take the cure. At one time a cable tramway climbed Bank Road and amenities such as the still popular riverside Hall Leys Park were created. By the start of World War 2, hydropathy was losing its attraction, and together with other smaller establishments that had grown around the sunny hillside of Matlock Bank, Smedley's Hydro eventually closed in 1955, only to be saved by the County Council.

Today Matlock is a thriving little town with many attractions, ranging from a good selection of shops, reasonably priced restaurants and cafés, a swimming pool and that rarity in a small town, a well supported cinema. The park has well-maintained tennis courts, bowling and putting greens, a small boating lake, miniature railway and a children's play area which includes a paddling pool. A single track railway, all that is left of the once mighty Midland Railway, still links Matlock to the main line at Derby and Peak Rail's ambitious plan to reopen the line northwards has its terminus at Riverside Halt, upstream of Matlock station.*

* On Boxing Day Matlock's annual raft race attracts both eccentric and serious competitors who manage to stave off hypothermia in the cause of charitable fund raising. Starting upstream of Matlock Bridge, the race finishes at Cromford Meadows.

High above the town the ruins of Riber Castle, another of Smedley's attempts to establish Matlock as a spa, now houses the **Riber Wildlife Park** which specialises in European birds and animals. Such is the success of the zoo's breeding programme, that lynx have been sent from Riber to re-establish these beautiful cats in Spanish Pyrenean national parks. To the rear of the castle, **Riber Hall** now an internationally renowned hotel and restaurant, dates from Elizabethan times.

Riber Wildlife Park
Rare, endangered and domesticated animals. Open all year.

The land falls steeply below Riber to the straggling village of Starkholmes, then rises again to the summit of the dramatic 350 ft limestone precipice of **High Tor**. Footpaths and open topped caves, make it an ideal place to explore and picnic, or simply to admire the wide ranging views. Paths over High Tor can be linked to

others on the opposite side of the valley but rock climbers claim the steep face of the tor as their own, and at its foot, canoeists can enjoy the white water slalom course either day or night.

Facing High Tor summit across the deep gorge, and almost hidden in woodland, St John's Chapel of Ease

Top: Matlock's Boxing Day Raft Race.
Above: Riber Hall .

High Tor and Heights of Abraham Walk p 162

High Tor and Riber Castle from the Heights of Abraham.

looks as though it was transported from Bavaria. Now disused it was once a private chapel built by Sir John Dawber, and was patronised by fashionable visitors to Smedley's Hydro.

Ever since thermal water was discovered in 1681 beneath what is now the New Bath Hotel, **Matlock Bath** has been a popular venue for visitors. Late Georgian frontages now house shops and cafés along the gently curving riverside road and across the river carefully engineered woodland paths climb the wooded hillside. The Pavilion no longer dispenses water from its elegant marble fountain, but the building is still used for dances and as a conference centre, with the ground floor as the home of the award winning 'hands on' **Peak District Mining Museum**. Covering 2000 years of Derbyshire lead mining history, it houses a giant water pressure engine resurrected from a local mine, manually operated pumps and easy to follow geological displays, but the main attraction is the cleverly reproduced group of mining shafts, just wide enough for children, but where grown ups get embarrassingly stuck! Entrance tickets to the museum also give access to the nearby **Temple Mine**, an abandoned lead mine worked until recently for the fluorspa ignored by earlier miners.

Peak District Mining Museum
Open all year.

Filling a suntrap on the wooded hillside above the mine is **Gulliver's Kingdom** where an entrance ticket allows free use of all the rides, making a visit an exciting

Gulliver's Kingdom
Fantasy theme park for young families.

day out for all the family. Another attraction is the **Matlock Bath Aquarium** on South Parade where, along with the usual tanks of tropical fish, voracious Khoi carp live in an old thermally fed swimming pool. The aquarium also has a tantalisingly lifelike display of hologram pictures.

One of the free visual features of a visit to Matlock Bath is the scores of expensive motorbikes parked along the road on most fine weekends. Another free event is the annual Venetian Fête held throughout the autumn when decorated boats paddle up and down the river from the imaginatively lit **Riverside Gardens**. Firework displays are also held on certain weekends.

Matlock Bath is a popular motorcyclists' venue (above left); the Fish Pond (above right) and the Riverside Gardens (below), are but a few of the attractions.

Matlock Bath Aquarium
Includes hologram gallery, petrifying well and gemstone collection.

Main line expresses no longer stop at Matlock Bath's Swiss chalet-style station, but it is still used by the local Matlock to Derby service. Built in 1849 to a design by Joseph Paxton, head gardener at Chatsworth, it now houses **Whistlestop**, the permanent exhibition centre for the Derbyshire Wildlife Trust. A

Heights of Abraham
Open daily Easter to
October.

cable car starting in woodland at the foot of High Tor a little way beyond the station, climbs to the **Heights of Abraham**, Matlock Bath's major attraction. Here there are woodland walks, the Treetops Restaurant and two well illuminated caverns where lead was first mined in Roman times, and where in the **Rutland Cavern** an animated model of an old miner explains his lifestyle. Climb the **Victoria Prospect Tower**, built to commemorate Queen Victoria's Diamond Jubilee, for one of the finest viewpoints in the area.

When Richard Arkwright was driven out of his native Lancashire by those who saw his invention of the mechanised spinning frame as a threat to their livelihood, he built his first mill in Nottingham, using horse power, but chose Cromford as the ideal place to build his water-powered cotton mill.***** Due to concern about the possibilty of attack from outsiders, **Cromford Mill** became the fortress-like structure which stands on Mill Lane. Success followed and in 1783 he built Masson Mill whose original Venetian windowed structure is still central to the complex currently undergoing redevelopment beside the A6. Eventually Arkwright mills were built where there was sufficient water power, at Ashbourne, Bakewell, Cressbrook and Wirksworth, as well as in Lanarkshire.

*Originally a wig maker, Richard Arkwright had regularly visited the village on buying expeditions for hair, and knew the locals were skilled stocking knitters. This, combined with a plentiful water supply to drive his mill, prompted his decision to build in rural Cromford in 1771.

Cromford Mill
Open daily, free entrance
to site. Charge for
guided tours.

Today Arkwright's original mill is slowly coming back to life under the auspices of the Arkwright Society. Conducted tours led by knowledgeable guides explain the layout and history of the mill, and together with a factory shop specialising in woollens, craft shops and a small café, a visit evokes the early days of the Industrial Revolution.

Cromford existed as an industrial village long before Arkwright arrived and converted it into a model village to house his employees. The older houses are mostly three-storied, with the upper floor once used by stocking knitting frame workers; many of these old houses, built in terraces had inter-connecting doors on their upper floors, creating galleries where operatives could quickly go to the aid of their colleagues.

Arkwright built North Street to the left of the Wirksworth road beyond the village centre, and where his son Richard later erected a school. Most of the shops opened in Arkwright's time can still be traced, even though no longer used for their original purpose. The

Greyhound Hotel in Cromford's market place was originally built to accommodate world-wide visitors who came to view the marvels of Arkwright's invention. Alison Uttley's *Our Village*, published by Scarthin Books, brings to life Cromford as it was around 1900, when the mill was fully operating.

Knighted in 1786, Arkwright built **Willersley Castle** to confirm his success but the original structure burned

Top: Heights of Abraham cable car.
Below: Cromford Mill Pond.

Cromford Canal: High Peak Junction (top); Leawood Pumping Station (below).

down, and he died in 1792 before it was rebuilt. Today the castle which overlooks a curving sweep of the River Derwent, is used as a holiday and conference centre by the Methodist Guild. It was his family who built the mock gothic church that stands between the mill and the castle and paid for the series of murals decorating the chancel walls.

Cromford Bridge dates from the 15th century, but there has been a river crossing there possibly since Roman times. It was once protected by a chapel, but only the foundations remain beside an 18th-century fishing pavilion (restored in 1968), with the inscription, *Piscatoribus Sacrum* over its door.

Realising the need for efficient transport, Arkwright was one of the instigators of the **Cromford Canal**, the then most efficient means of carrying goods. Although now only navigable as far as the 200 yards long aqueduct crossing of the River Derwent below Lea Bridge, the canal became a link with the East Midlands and the rest of the countrywide canal network. If only to enjoy a pleasant waterside walk, a canal offers an interesting insight into the industrial archaeology of the area, as well as enjoying the unspoilt wildlife . Fed partly by a culvert draining old lead mines beyond Cromford, the canal also relied upon water pumped from the River Derwent. Steam-operated **Leawood Pumping House** with its distinctive chimney has been restored and is run on advertised days. Downstream of the aqueduct, woodland and abandoned canal have become a haven for wildlife under the care of the Derbyshire Wildlife Trust.

A swing bridge allows access to a group of single-storied buildings on the opposite side of the canal. This is **High Peak Junction**, the southern end of a unique railway line across the limestone plateau of the Peak District. After the completion of the Peak Forest Canal in 1800, which had its terminus in Whaley Bridge, a number of ambitious, but impractical schemes were devised to link it with the Cromford Canal. All were abandoned in favour of a railway, but as it was built by the canal engineer Josiah Jessop, the stations were called wharfs and it climbed gradients by inclines, the steepest of which were aided by stationary steam engines. Only the **Middleton Top engine** remains and beautifully restored, it is 'steamed' on advertised days throughout the summer. The 33 mile line, operated from 1830 until 1967, is now used as far as its junction with the Tissington Trail as the walking, riding and cycling, all-weather traffic free **High Peak Trail**. Bicycles can be hired at Middleton Top, or Parsley Hay.

> **Middleton Top Visitor Centre, High Peak Trail**
> Bicycle hire, information centre. Open February to November. Check times –
> Tel: 01629 823204

A walk which starts by following the canal as far as High Peak Junction wharf, climbs steeply via the incline through natural woodland, past the remains of a winding engine house to the dramatic gritstone outcrop of **Black Rocks**. Before turning right below the rocks spend a little time investigating the partly restored ruins of the lead smelter where ore mined beneath Black Rocks was processed. The route then follows narrow back ways into Cromford, avoiding the heavily used Cromford Hill road where lorries laden with limestone from nearby quarries ease their way down the steep hill past cottages once the homes of frame knitters.

> **Cromford and Black Rocks Walk**
> p 163

The A5012 Newhaven road from Cromford follows Griffe Grange Valley, but mostly it is known as the Via Gellia.* Heavy lorries make pedestrian access to the gorge almost impossible, but the end result is something of a blessing in disguise. Wildflowers such as

> ** The Via Gellia was first built by the Gell family of Hopton Hall near Carsington, who gave it the fanciful Roman sounding title.*

Thirteen circular steps lead to Bonsall Cross.

Scarthin Bookshop
New, secondhand and antiquarian books.
Open daily.

Good Luck Mine
Tel: 01629 583834
for details of tours.

lily of the valley are no longer picked, they were considered a commercial crop at one time, and the valley sides are now given over to nature.

Cromford mill pond with its backing of old cottages is a popular vantage point, especially along almost traffic-free Scarthin Lane where a browse in **Scarthin Bookshop** makes an alternative attraction. Water feeding the pond comes via an overshot waterwheel beside a basket works, and opposite it a small shop specialises in hand made quilts.

A cottage built from tufa, naturally reconstituted limestone, is the only habitation along the narrowest part of the dale, and on the hillside above is Mountain Cottage where Eastwood born author DH Lawrence lived for a year. Overlooking the Via Gellia below Lawrence's cottage is the **Good Luck Mine**, a preserved lead mine which can be explored by pre-arranged guided tours. For details of booking please check with the Peak District Mining Museum at Matlock Bath.

A one-time pub, The Pig of Lead, a link with the bygone industry, marks the side road climbing to **Bonsall**. At the centre of the village a ball-topped medieval cross above thirteen circular steps overlooks the King's Head, established in 1677, and close by is the old manor house dating from the same era. The church has even older foundations laid in the 13th and 14th centuries; of special interest are the gargoyles surrounding the battlemented spire and inside are fragments of ancient coffin stones and several fine brasses. Village wells are dressed in July, and for Bonfire Night the village specialises in creating almost lifelike guys.

A group of villages built along a south facing slope above the Derwent beyond Cromford, marks the end of this chapter. Away from the more popular tourist areas, nevertheless they have much to offer, especially when the A6 and Matlock become overcrowded.

The road from Cromford winds its way beside the river to **Lea Bridge** where Smedley's Mill Shop sells woollens manufactured in the adjacent mill. **Dethick**, the most northerly village in this group, is much smaller than in Tudor times when one of its inhabitants, Anthony Babington misguidedly tried to free Mary Queen of Scots from Wingfield Manor, and lost his head as a result. All that remains of the village is a couple of farms and a tiny church standing lonely in a field. **Lea** straggles across the hillside and has a pub and a restaurant specialising in home-made ice cream, but most visitors head for **Lea Rhododendron Gardens**. The magnificent collection of rhododendrons and

Lea Rhododendron Gardens
Open daily mid-March to end of July.

Lea Rhododendron Gardens are a blaze of colour from May to July.

National Tramway Museum, Crich.

azaleas, the work of four generations of the Tye family, is set in an ancient pine shaded quarry where Roman querns have been found. The gardens are at their finest from May to July, especially after a run of sunny weather.

Florence Nightingale returned unheralded to Lea Hurst, her birthplace in **Holloway**, after caring for wounded soldiers in the Crimea. The house is now used as an old people's home, but is opened to the puplic for special events. Below the house a footpath passes a private estate where llamas can often be seen grazing alongside red deer.

* The ridge top village of Crich with its scattered groups of stone cottages built around tiny squares, is frequently used as the setting for the TV drama, Peak Practice where it is better known as Cardale.

The road climbs out of Holloway, through woodland where occasional breaks in the trees give southerly views along the Derwent, to **Crich**.* The church dates from the 12th and 14th centuries and is built on a high point overlooking widespread views of the Peak District as well as the north Midlands plain. Limestone making its last appearance hereabouts, is still quarried. Topping the quarry, **Crich Stand**, the memorial to the Sherwood Foresters who fell in two World Wars, is unexpectedly a lighthouse. The first Sunday in July is marked by a pilgrimage to the Stand.

An abandoned section of the quarry is now used by the **National Tramway Museum**, a collection of vintage trams from all over the world. For the cost of an old penny (or halfpenny for children), which is given on entry to the museum, you can spend all day wallowing in the nostalgia of riding up and down a mile or so of scenic track, high above the Derwent Valley. Along with the operating trams, the museum has an extensive indoor section, video theatre, workshops, restored buildings and special advertised events throughout the year. During the run-up to Christmas there are illuminated events and at other times anyone arriving in a vintage car gets in free!

National Tramway Museum
For details of special events Tel: 01773 852565

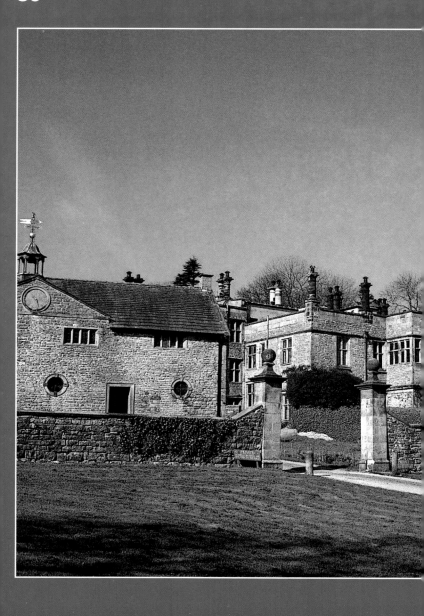

The Dove and Manifold Valleys

On their journey southwards the rivers Dove and Manifold flow through increasingly lush farmland in their infancy, then rush dramatically through deep and wooded dales whose beauty has been cherished for generations. Strange rock formations overlook deep pools where trout and grayling hide, testing angler's skills. The once grazed valley sides are, with the help of careful tree clearance, a haven for wildflowers and birdlife. Sleepy villages where time is still measured in centuries, dot the surrounding uplands, focal points for dairy farms.

Tissington Hall, home of the Fitzherberts since Elizabethan times.

Washgate packhorse bridge, Upper Dove.

While both the Dove and Manifold rivers begin as springs rising within a couple of miles of each other below Axe Edge, their characters are completely different. The Dove seems impatient to become the trout stream made famous by the 17th-century angler and writer, Izaac Walton and his impecunious friend, Charles Cotton. On the other hand the Manifold wanders lazily in its upper reaches before entering the gorge it has carved deep into the limestone, and where it frequently disappears underground. The two rivers join below Thorpe, the new river continuing the name Dove all the way to its confluence with the Trent.

The Dove Valley

Three miles south-west of the outskirts of Buxton, a side turning on the left away from the A53 Leek road, drops down from Axe Edge to the tiny hillside hamlet of **Brand Top**. A well near one of the farms still flows with crystal clear water, but more importantly it is the acknowledged source of the **River Dove**. Rapidly carving a deep channel through the underlying gritstone shales, the river is bordered by remote moorland farms, homes of beef and sheep farmers.

The moors once echoed to the jingle and clipclop of pack ponies. Many of the ancient routes, used for

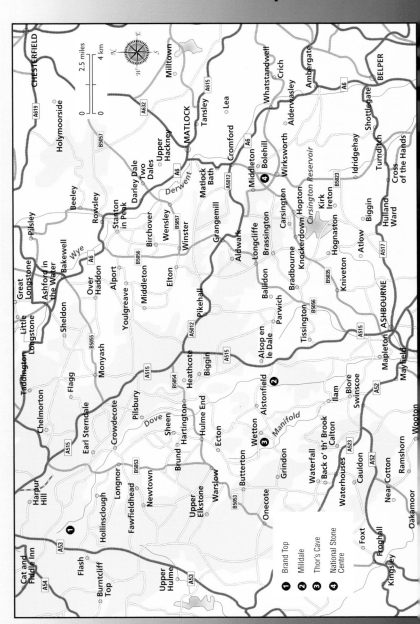

A bright late winter day in Hollinsclough.

Brand Top Walk p 163

* A small museum of old rural artifacts garnered from the surrounding farms can be seen at special, locally advertised events.

carrying goods before the railways took over, can still be traced as narrow unsurfaced lanes. A walk around Upper Dovedale starts at Brand Top and uses one of the old packhorse ways. At Washgate, the Dove is crossed by the graceful 21 foot span of a packhorse bridge, still with its original 4ft 6in apart parapets built low enough not to obstruct the panniers of the packhorses.

Hollinsclough barely scrapes into the category of a village, but makes up for its lack of size by a thriving community association intent on keeping many of its folk memories and traditions alive.* The village has two chapels, and a rarity in many rural areas, a thriving junior school. The modern school is tucked away behind its 19th-century predecessor, the Frank Wheldon School. The imposing building is topped by a unique wooden 'dove cote' bell tower which once summoned children from the outlying moorland farms. It now finds use as the Michael Hutchinson Outdoor Centre. Directly opposite Hollinsclough the series of shapely hills, Hollins, Chrome, Parkhouse, Hitter and High Wheeldon, some of the few true peaks in the Peak District, are the remains of ancient coral reefs once washed by the waters of a shallow tropical sea. High Wheeldon is owned by the National Trust in memory of the men of Staffordshire and Derbyshire who fell during the Second World War.

North of this line of hills, **Earl Sterndale's** inn the Quiet Woman, to the annoyance of feminists depicts a headless woman. The 19th-century church accidentally bombed during the war, stands on the site of a much earlier chapel, and has a crudely shaped font thought to date from Saxon times.

Glutton Bridge marks the Staffordshire and Derbyshire boundary.

Oddly named **Glutton Bridge**, a cluster of farms and cottages, sits astride the road from Buxton to Longnor. On the opposite side of the hill and downstream along the Dove, **Crowdecote** was used as a resting place by packhorse drivers in time gone by, their memory retained by the name of the cosy Packhorse Inn.

Downstream from Crowdecote and only reached by footpaths, a series of mounds and earthen walls turn out to be the remnant of a motte and bailey dating from Norman times and known as **Pilsbury Castle**. An interpretive plaque explains a little of its history. **Sheen's** church spire overtops the skyline opposite, on the Staffordshire side of the Dove. A linear village of sturdy farms and cottages with pleasant gardens, particularly so in Spring, a visit is well worth the effort, especially if linked to a visit to its pub, the Staffordshire Knot, a little inn with a reputation for good food.

The next village along the Dove is **Hartington**, a popular centre for exploring the upper reaches of the

At one time a weekly Wednesday market and three annual fairs were held on Hartington's wide village green, but today the village concentrates on catering for tourists while remaining the focal point of the local farming community.

Hartington Cheese Shop, sells locally produced cheeses.

main dale.* Two old established inns sit to one side of the square alongside shops selling everything from sheepskins and tweeds, to hand-made terracotta pots and garden ornaments. Cafés and a second-hand book shop make useful stopping places after a walk in the dales, but the one attraction to save until last is a visit to the **Cheese Shop**. Milk from local dairy farms is converted into the famous Blue Stilton and other types of cheese by Mendip Dairy Crest at their dairy beyond the village duck pond.

Hartington was in its small way linked with major historical events. A one-day battle during the Civil War in the 1640s saw 600 Royalist Cavaliers slaughtered by Oliver Cromwell's troops. Spent bullets from the skirmish are still turning up beneath the plough on Hartington Moor. Bonnie Prince Charlie spent a night here during his long march on London in 1745, only to abandon his quest at Derby after hearing, incorrectly as it turned out, that his enemies were nearby. Tradition has it that the Jacobite prince lodged with the Batemans at Hartington Hall, the lovely gabled hall on the hill opposite the church. Built in 1611 on even older foundations, the hall is now a popular youth hostel where thousands of young people have been introduced to the delights of the nearby countryside.

The village church dedicated to St Giles, was built in the 14th century, but probably on earlier foundations. Around and inside the church stand remnants of Saxon stones, monuments to the Bateman family who lived in the village for something like 400 years, and traces of medieval wall paintings. A coffin stone reputed to be in memory of Margaret de Ferrers shows her head and in her hands she holds her heart.

Charles Cotton the angling friend of Izaak Walton lived close by at Beresford Hall. Nothing remains of the hall except a fishing temple (on private land, but visible from within Beresford Dale), where he and Walton discussed the finer points of their sport. There is a cave in this dale where the frequently impecunious Cotton hid from his creditors.

Hartington Well Dressings held on the second Saturday in September.

Hartington dresses its wells during the village Wakes Week, a tradition which only began in 1980. This and other events are advertised in the local and national park press.

Trains once ran between Ashbourne and Buxton, and Hartington had its own station. Never a profitable line, it fell to the Beeching Axe, but is now part of the popular Tissington Trail. A car park on the site of Hartington Station makes a useful starting point for easy cycle rides or short walks along the trail. Cycles may be hired at **Parsley Hay** which is just off the A515 Buxton to Ashbourne road a little to the north of Hartington.

London-bound mail coaches once stopped beside the A515 at the now abandoned Georgian roadside inn at Newhaven, but nearby Carriages Restaurant is its modern counterpart. Moving back towards Dovedale, **Biggin** serves the needs of local farmers with its regular sheep and cattle markets, and has one pub.

The valley of the Dove below Hartington while classed by most as **Dovedale**, is however a series of linked dales with only the last section taking this title or what the Ordnance Survey prefers to use, Dove Dale.

Carved deeply into the surrounding limestone, Dovedale has been the premier beauty spot of the Peak District for centuries.* Its very title conjures a picture of sylvan loveliness, but the name has nothing to do with

Summer in Wolfscote Dale, one of the linking dales of Dovedale.

Parsley Hay Cycle Hire
Open all year.

* Famous visitors to Dovedale in the past included Dr Johnson, William Morris and Mark Twain; the French philosopher Jean Jacques Rousseau visited it while exiled at nearby Wootton Hall; the poet Byron even compared it with Greece and Switzerland.

The George at Alstonfield makes a welcome venue for anyone exploring the countryside around Dovedale.

Biggin and Iron Tors Walk p 163

Hartington and its Dales Walk p 163

* The word pike has nothing to do with the predatory fish of that name, but is a corruption of 'Spike', an apt description of the tall rock within the pool.

peace and comes from the Celtic *dubh*, meaning dark, a description of its waters, especially after heavy rain on the high moors of Axe Edge.

The dale can be explored at any time of the year, but late Spring is probably best when the trees and wildflowers are at their finest. The river meanders through open meadows into the first section, **Beresford Dale**. Accessible only by a footpath and now mostly mud free since the National Trust began its policy of footpath improvement, Dovedale can be explored either by a continuous walk along its riverside path, or by any of a number of circular walks from nearby villages. The walks described on page 163 are just a sample of those possible.

A field path from Hartington enters wooded Beresford Dale then quickly descends towards the river, with a passing glimpse of the fishing temple, then over a little bridge beside Pike Pool* so loved by Izaak Walton and his younger friend Charles Cotton. The next is **Wolfscote Dale**, less wooded than its northern neighbour and where tiny semi-alpine flowers cling to crevices in the limestone crags. A side dale **Biggin Dale**, is equally rugged and leads to the village of the same name.

The valley begins to deepen and limestone is more and more apparent all the way past Iron Tors and its unnamed side dale. Long dead industry gave the name to **Milldale** where a narrow road crosses the valley below Shining Tor on the eastern bank with Alstonfield on the opposite heights. Despite its one-time industry, Milldale village, the only habitation within the valley, is now a tranquil riverside hamlet only visited by local traffic and walkers. Traces of the two mills which brought industry to this tranquil spot can still be seen; Lode Mill upstream beside the Alstonfield road prepared lead ore for smelting, and closer to the village proper is the Ochre Mill which was powered by water diverted from the Dove by way of a channel, or leat. A millstone once used for grinding the ochre pigment lies near the riverbank. Pack horses crossed the river by the narrow, single-spanned bridge opposite Lode Mill, called **Viator's Bridge**.*(1) This makes a good place to start a walk which visits the shallow riverside caves known as Dove Holes, and also Hanson Grange once a monastic grange farm.

High above the dale, but linked to it by ancient roads and trackways, **Alstonfield** has seen the coming and going of travellers over the centuries. Although the Ordnance Survey spell it Alstonefield, the locals prefer Alstonfield, without an 'e'. The confused County Council used both versions on roadsigns at the village boundaries. Once an important junction of packhorseways, it is now used by walkers and cyclists, who still make for the cosy hospitality of the George Inn. A local artist Jean Goodwin exhibits local scenes at her gallery near the village green, and there is also a small but well-stocked craft shop. On the right, just outside the village on the Ilam road, a privately owned museum, the **Hope House Costume Museum** and Restoration Workshop holds a collection of around 300 costumes and accessories, covering the period between 1840 and the 1970s.

Walton and Cotton worshipped at Alstonfield's parish church in the beautifully panelled and canopied pew. The church is built on Saxon foundations and has several pre-Norman crosses and coffin stones.*(2)

(1) 'Viator's Bridge is named after a fictitious conversation between Izaak Walton (Viator) and Charles Cotton (Piscator), in Walton's Compleat Angler the 17th-century angler's handbook. In it he describes the Dove as, "the finest river that I ever saw and the fullest of fish".

Viator's Bridge Walk p 164

(2) The oddest relic in Alstonfield Church is the economically worded inscription on the double decker pulpit which states, "Be faithful and etc., and I will give thee a crown etc." No doubt the carpenter was in a hurry when he carved that!

Hope House Costume Museum
Appointments only
Tel: 01335 310318

Viator's Bridge, Milldale.

The Stepping Stones in Dovedale.

* There is no record of any star-crossed lovers jumping from the summit of the latter rock, but in 1761 the Dean of Clougher in Ulster, a Mr Langton managed to fall from it together with his horse. He was killed, but his young lady travelling companion was saved when her long hair caught in the branches of a tree.

Below Milldale the wooded valley enters its finest scenery, first 'discovered' during the enthusiastic search for romanticism in the 19th century. The river has carved deeply into the limestone, creating dramatic rock formations and shallow caves. Dove Holes offer thoughts of prehistoric shelter, and downstream, Lion Rock has the shape of the noble beast's head. Above it high on the Derbyshire side of the dale, **Reynard's Cave** was used as a dwelling in Romano-British times. Many of the outcrops and spires were given fanciful titles by Victorian tourists, and so we now have Ilam Rock, Jacob's Ladder, the Twelve Apostles and Dovedale Castle on the west, or Staffordshire side of Dovedale, and Tissington Spires and Lovers' Leap* on the other, the Derbyshire side.

Below Lovers' Leap a short stretch of water meadow leads to the best known part of Dovedale. Here the **Stepping Stones** create an often photographed riverscape backed by the lofty portals of **Bunster Hill** to the west and **Thorpe Cloud** to the east. Both hills are the remnants of ancient coral reefs once teeming with aquatic plants and animals whose fossilised remains can still be seen, especially around the summit of Thorpe Cloud. The word '*cloud*' comes from the Old English word *'clud'*, meaning a rock or hill. As with most of Dovedale, Thorpe Cloud is owned by the National Trust. The river is joined by the Manifold a half mile downstream of the Stepping Stones car park, their united waters continuing as the Dove. A 6½ mile walk starts at the Dovedale car park, climbs the side of Bunster Hill, then joins the river by Ilam Rock and follows the dale downstream back to the car park by way of the Stepping Stones.

Thorpe village sits slightly to one side of the road to Dovedale, an unsophisticated place despite its closeness to the dale. Although its church was much 'improved' in Victorian times, many of its Norman and 14th-century parts are still visible. 'Improvements' partly obliterated the 17th-century tomb of John Milward which juts out of the chancel wall. In front are tiny figures of two daughters dressed in gowns with embroidered bodices, and two sons in cloaks and wide-topped riding boots. Both these sons were soldiers, one a colonel in the service of King Charles I.

The natural arch of Reynard's Cave, Dovedale.

During the turnpike era, a road from Cheadle in Staffordshire to Chesterfield, crossed the Dove below Thorpe by the long and substantial Coldwall Bridge. Proving too steep for later traffic the road was abandoned and is now a pleasant green lane, with the bridge used only by farm vehicles and walkers between Thorpe and Blore.

Dovedale Walk p 164

The busy A515 on its way from Ashbourne to Buxton seems to ignore **Fenny Bentley**. This most southerly village in the Peak District National Park lies mostly to the west of the road, but the Old Hall is visible to passing cars. The moated house is built around what looks like a pele tower, or possibly the gatehouse of an earlier building. It was once the home of Thomas Beresford who in 1415 fought the French alongside Henry V at the Battle of Agincourt. He and his wife are buried in the 19th-century restoration of a 14th-century village church, with their effigies completely bundled in marble shrouds. Their descendants attend an annual reunion of the Beresford Family Society.

Well dressing in Tissington (above) where the children learn the art of well dressing early (below).

Tissington Hall, open June and July on advertised days **Tissington Well Dressings**, held in May.

A mile or so to the north and east of the A515, a splendid avenue of limes leads to **Tissington**, considered by many to be the most attractive village in the Peak. The village spreads gently away from its pond, but the Norman church is the real focal point. **Tissington Hall** is Jacobean, dating from 1610, but with Georgian extensions. Tissington, hall and village, has been owned by the Fitzherbert family since Elizabethan times, and their care ensures the village remains unspoilt by modern development. The car park at the old railway station above the village is on the Tissington Trail, and makes a suitable starting point for easy cycle rides along the almost level track. Tissington dresses its five attractive wells, and also the Children's Well, for Ascension Day, one of the earliest in the Peak to do so. According to Peakland folk lore, the custom of well dressing began in Tissington, a custom which grew from simple floral tributes to the complex art form of today.

The Manifold Valley

Unlike its sister the Dove, no single place can be identified as the true birthplace of the **Manifold**. Several streams rise from the bleak shales of Axe Edge and soon join to make the Manifold. If one must be singled out as the parent spring then perhaps it is that which rises near the Travellers' Rest on Flash Head. Few if any tributaries join from the east, but several including the Hamps, the Manifold's major side stream, flow from the west. At one time there were plans to flood the wide shallow basin below Longnor, but fortunately they were abandoned in the face of local opposition. The underlying rocks are shales as far as Hulme End. Here the river begins to meet limestone, a rock so porous that further down the dale, the Manifold frequently disappears underground, only to resurface near Ilam.

Longnor's church tower from one of its narrow streets.

Tiny farm-based villages dot the moors with **Longnor** traditionally their focal point. The village sits on a high ledge above the Manifold and is where until recent memory farmers brought their produce and animals for sale. The market house with its scale of charges above the door overlooks a cobbled square. No longer used for its original purpose, the building now houses a craft workshop and café. Classified as a Conservation Area, Longnor is one of those places where quiet wandering down narrow back alleys often leads to the discovery of delightful cottages and scenes. The village was once part of the Crewe and Harpur estate, a fact highlighted by the name of one of the group of inns surrounding the market square.*

The decline in village population which troubles many upland villages has been halted in Longnor with the creation of a thriving rural industrial estate. An abandoned chapel now finds a new use as a dolls' hospital.

A complex pattern of moorland roads turns east then south from the A53 Leek road. One of them leaves the main road beyond the Royal Cottage Inn where Bonnie Prince Charlie rested on his long march to and from Derby. This road, never dropping much below 1400 feet, winds its way south across the Morridge moors where the remote Mermaid Inn is the only habitation for several

Longnor Two Valleys Walk p 164

* Although Longnor church was rebuilt in the 18th century, it stands on foundations at least 800 years old. Look for the tombstone of William Billinge who lies buried in the graveyard, and if we are to believe records of the day, was 112 when he died in 1791. A soldier who fought under the Duke of Marlborough, he faced death so many times in action, that he believed death had overlooked him.

miles. As befits such a remote spot, a nearby pool is said to be the haunt of a mermaid who drags the unwary to their doom. The inn once looked after the needs of coal miners who worked the shallow pits on the surrounding moors, but now offers a very high standard of food and wines.*(1) A field almost opposite the Mermaid is used by the Staffordshire Gliding Club as their airstrip.

(1) For several days either side of mid-summers's day, the sun when viewed from the Mermaid appears to set twice when it passes behind Hen Cloud to the north west.

The Elkstones Upper and Lower, seem to hide within a fold of the hills below Morridge. The church in Upper Elkstone is a simple towerless and aisleless structure, where box pews and round-headed sash windows indicate its Georgian ancestry. Warslow Brook flows past the two hamlets, but curiously by-passes the village from which it takes its name. **Warslow** like Longnor, is a focal point for the surrounding farms and where moorland dwelling children are educated to secondary level. Again like Longnor, Warslow was a Crewe estate village, with the church built in 1820 by Sir George Crewe of Calke Abbey near Melbourne south of Derby. Along with later improvements, the church features Morris stained glass windows. Sir George also built Warslow Hall as a shooting box about $1\frac{1}{2}$ miles north of the village along the B5058, Longnor road.

Moving back towards the main valley, **Hulme End** was, between 1904 and 1934, the northern terminus of the Leek and Manifold Valley Light Railway. Built initially to carry milk and produce from what was then a remote farming area, the railway became a popular way for passengers to reach the delights of the Manifold Valley. Never economical, its demise came with improved road transport. Never again will the primrose liveried carriages drawn by lovingly burnished steam locomotives resplendent with massive headlamps, pass along the valley. Since 1937 the track of the old railway has been a paved footpath, making it easy for even the most infirm to explore the inner recesses of the Manifold Valley.

(2) Falling output and declining profits led to the closure of the complex of mines on Ecton Hill in the early 19th century, but not before a staggering £2,500,000 profit had been made.

A large hill dominates the landscape immediately to the south of Hulme End. This is **Ecton Hill**, a hill which today gives little hint of the fortunes won and lost beneath its green slopes. Copper and lead were mined here for over three centuries but all that remains of the once intensive industry are scattered piles of rubble and a drainage outflow close to the valley road, together with the restored Agent's House, (private).*(2)

While the footpath continues to follow the old railway, the riverside road leaves the valley at **Wettonmill**. There is a café here and a small car park, making it easy to explore the valley, or maybe venture further afield by climbing up to **Thor's Cave** where our prehistoric ancestors once sheltered.

Thor's Cave Walk
p 164

At Wettonmill, the river makes the first of its disappearing acts beneath the fissured limestone, or 'swallets', only reappearing finally below Ilam Hall, about seven miles downstream.

Three villages sit high above the Manifold. To the west, **Butterton** and **Grindon** are peaceful little places, the spires of their churches the only distantly visible evidence of their whereabouts. Life is quiet, but during the Great Blizzard of 1947, tragedy struck when an aircraft crashed while dropping emergency supplies, killing all six crew. Opposite and above the eastern valley

Wettonmill bridge in the Manifold Valley.

rim, **Wetton** was the home of Samuel Carrington, who, together with his friend Thomas Bateman of Middleton-by-Youlgreave discovered many Romano-British and Neolithic remains around Wetton.

A steep hairpin-bended road from Grindon crosses the river at Weags Bridge. It was here the old railway left the Manifold to follow the winding curves of the River Hamps. The side valley makes a sharp turn at **Waterhouses**, almost doubling back on itself, away from the busy A523 Leek /Ashbourne road and back into the national park. From the village, the national park boundary follows a minor road climbing steadily on the Morridge heights. To the right of this road the B5053 to Hartington road passes by the mellow stone village of **Onecote**.

Bicycles can be hired at Waterhouses, making it an ideal starting point to explore the easy track along the Hamps and Manifold valleys. Almost hidden and well

Waterhouses Cycle Hire
Brown End Farm and Old Station car park. See signs in village.

Throwley Hall is based on an old pele (defensive) tower.

away from the main road is **Waterfall** with its single pub also serving the quaintly named satellite hamlet called **Back o' th' Brook**, which completes the little known cluster of unpretentious villages in the quiet corner of the Peak to the west of the Manifold.

Limestone based soils support rich meadows where wildflowers bloom on land 'unimproved' by chemical fertilisers. The valley sides above the Manifold have been farmed by countless generations whose ancestors built the sturdy houses such as Castern Hall and its neighbour above the west bank of the dale, **Throwley Hall** where the remains of a pele tower stand amidst the slightly more modern buildings.

Founded by the Celtic missionary, St Bertram, **Ilam** marks the last mile of the Manifold before its waters, resurging nearby after their long journey underground, soon mingle with those of the Dove. Ilam is a good example of an estate village. Although there was a hall and village founded in medieval times, the present village dates from the mid 1800s. It was here that the shipping magnate Jesse Watts-Russell and the architect Gilbert Scott planned to create an estate competing with the Earl of Shrewsbury's Alton Towers. Surrounding himself with a gingerbread-style village, he built a massive Gothic hall and proceeded to live the life of a country gentleman.

* St Bertram is supposed to have lived in the shallow cave where part of the underground waters reappear and his well where he baptised converts is on the slopes of Bunster Hill. The attractive bridge in the grounds of Ilam Hall below the church dating from the 19th century, is also dedicated to St Bertram.

The Watts-Russell family only lived at Ilam for a couple of generations, but left their mark on this corner of the dales. Not only the hall and village, but the church with its grandiose Chantry memorial to Russell's father-in-law, David Watts, was built at this time, the restoration of a much earlier building. Untouched though, is the shrine of St Bertram, once a place of pilgrimage.* St Bertram's Well can also be visited on a walk around lower Dovedale and the surrounding hillsides.

The 30ft mock-Eleanor memorial cross in the middle of the village, was to Jesse Watts-Russell's first wife,

who if folk memory is correct, was not over popular amongst the local tenantry.

Following a short life as a country hotel, Ilam Hall was sold and partly demolished in 1934 when the flour magnate Sir Robert McDougall bought it for the nation. Fortunately he saved a substantial portion of the hall, which together with the estate is now owned by the National Trust. Part of Sir Robert's instructions when he bought Ilam was that the hall was to be leased to the Youth Hostels Association. The grounds and woodland are laid out with walks, including the riverside Paradise Walk. *

An ideal centre for exploring both Dovedale and the Lower Manifold Valley, Ilam makes a pleasant start to a walk which passes the confluence of the two rivers.

Downstream of Ilam, the Manifold flows with the Dove, southwards through green pastures and secluded game woods, beyond the hilly confines of its youth and into a much wider valley. Two minor roads give access to this little known part of the Dove and the village of **Mapleton**, a village of mellow brick cottages opposite Okeover Hall on the Staffordshire side of the river. There is one pub in the village and a tea room-cum-post office advertising cream teas. Okeover Hall is private, but a public road from Mayfield crosses the deer park in front of the house.

The Watts-Russell Memorial Cross at Ilam is said to be based on an Eleanor Cross.

* Long a popular attraction, Ilam was visited by Dr Johnson and a stone table in an alcove above Paradise Walk can still be found where William Congreve wrote his bawdy play The Old Bachelor in 1693.

**Ilam Hall Walk
p 165**

Above: Ashbourne's Elizabethan Grammar school and St Oswald's Church (below).

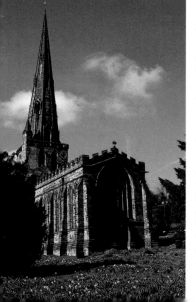

Ashbourne and the South East Peak

With the exception of Parwich, all the towns and villages described in this section lie just outside the south eastern boundary of the Peak District National Park. Probably because of this and despite the attraction of Carsington Water in their midst, they are comparatively little known and, as a result worthy of further exploration. Set amongst rolling farmland, the area where they lie is roughly bounded by the triangle of roads, the B5056 Grangemill to Ashbourne road, the A517 Belper road, and the A6 and A5012 respectively to the east and north.

The road sign on entering **Ashbourne** tells us that it is the 'Gateway to Dovedale', an accurate description for this busy market town. But there is more to Ashbourne than being simply a 'gateway'. The town centre around the cobbled market place, together with St John's Street and Compton, is lined with pleasant Georgian town houses; mostly converted into shops, but with many still fulfilling their original domestic purpose.

St Oswald's church is at the far end of the town, an indication that the town has moved eastwards over the centuries. One of the finest examples of the Early English style in the North Midlands, it is dominated by a 212 foot high tower and spire; inside are memorials to the rich and famous of the district.*(1) Try to visit St Oswald's in spring when the churchyard becomes a sea of bright yellow daffodils.

The Old Grammar School with its long row of mullioned windows and steep gables, was founded by the Cockaynes in 1585. It stands diagonally across the road from the church, and next to the school at number 61 is the Grey House. Almost opposite and adjacent to a group of alms houses is the 17th-century Mansion House where the lexicographer and traveller Dr Johnson frequently stayed when visiting his friend Dr Taylor. Next to them on the church side is the Old House, offering bed and breakfast, the only house along this part of the street open to the public.

Dr Johnson and his amanuensis James Boswell also stayed at the Green Man near the market place, where Boswell found it 'a very good inn' and its landlady 'a mighty civil gentlewoman'. His inn is no more, but the 'gallows' sign once linking it to the Black's Head Royal Hotel opposite is still a feature, commemorating the amalgamation of the two coaching inns in 1825. The still functioning coaching inn has taken its neighbour's title and is now known simply as the Green Man. A little further along the street is a shop selling Ashbourne gingerbread.*(2) Another famous product is Ashbourne Water bottled by Nestlé at their nearby factory.

A plaque on the side of a small terraced house in Sturston Road above Compton, tells us that it was the home of Catherine Booth, the wife of General William Booth, founder of the Salvation Army.

Bonnie Prince Charlie and his army came through Ashbourne in 1745, and possibly because of this, the town hosts a Highland Gathering each summer. Better known however, is the **Shrovetide Football** match when all sensible shop keepers board up their windows. At 2:00pm on Shrove Tuesday and the next day Ash Wednesday, a specially made cork-filled leather ball is 'thrown up' by a visiting personality. This then is the start of absolute mayhem when teams, consisting of

(1) One of the most touching memorials in St Oswald's Church is the white Carrara marble representation of five year old Penelope Booth by who died in 1793. It was a painting of her by Sir Joshua Reynolds that inspired Pears Soap's famous 'Bubbles' advert.

(2) Ashbourne Gingerbread was made, so they say, to a recipe left by French prisoners held captive in Ashbourne during the Napoleonic Wars.

Ashbourne Shrovetide Football
Annual, traditional football played in the streets.

Carsington Water.

hundreds owing allegiance either to the 'Upards' or 'Downards' (north or south of the Henmore Brook) part of the town, try to carry the ball back to their own goals three miles apart on the site of the old Clifton and Sturston mills. The river is no barrier, and play stops at 10:00pm. It is rare for more than a couple of goals to be scored in this game which has its links with an even more barbaric event played in pre-Christian times.

The A517 road to Belper follows a high ridge from Ashbourne and skirts **Hulland Ward**, a village where the view from the church tower takes in the Wrekin in Shropshire 40 miles away to the south west, and most of the dales and moors of the Peak to its north. Three miles further on is **Turnditch** overlooking the Ecclesbourne valley. Then north via quiet by-roads along this lovely valley is **Idridgehay** and 19th-century Alton Manor where annual garden parties are held on behalf of charitable causes.

Between **Kirk Ireton**, with its venerable old church and **Hognaston**, where the catering at the Red Lion is so good it is advisable to book beforehand, (Tel: (01335) 370396), the long curve of Carsington Water's dam fits

St James' Church, Brassington.

well into the landscape. Opened in 1992, the reservoir is unusual in that it is filled mainly in winter by water pumped from the River Derwent about 6½ miles away, then released in summer to provide supplies for the North Midlands. Sailing, windsurfing, rafting, canoeing and fishing facilities are available, together with mountain biking on the specially made 8 mile circuit, and are but a few of the many pleasures to be had on and around **Carsington Water**. Here too are picnic sites, restaurants, craft shops and a Visitor Centre where the story of water, and especially Carsington, is graphically explained.*

The reservoir takes its title from the nearby twin villages of **Carsington** and **Hopton**. They fit snugly beneath a steeply wooded hillside and the Miner's Arms tells of the occupations of men and women, who once lived in the jumble of limestone cottages. The church is 14th-century in origin and inside are memorials to the Gells of Hopton, a major landowning family in this part of the Peak.

A walk starts from the western end of the village and climbs a steep hillside dotted with the remains of countless abandoned mine shafts. The footpath makes its return from **Brassington** where yet another Miner's Arms once slaked the thirsts of miners who believed ale prevented lead poisoning. The grey limestone village is built on a series of terraces as though to catch the best of the sun. The church began its ministrations in

* A complete change from the old days when visitors were banned from going anywhere near reservoirs, Carsington has many extra features, such as the heavy black granite ball supported by water, rotating at the gentlest touch, to the modern 'henge' where many of its stones align with distant features.

Carsington Pasture Walk p 165

Even though the abandoned mine shafts are mostly made safe and capped by concrete slabs, take great care when venturing close to these relics of long dead industry.

* (1) At Brassington Church, try to find the small carved figure of a man with his hand on his heart, high on the wall of the tower. Its origin is unknown, but it is thought to be Saxon and put there by the Norman builders.

Norman times, with additions made between the 13th and 15th centuries, an indication of the once prosperous nature of the lead mining district.*(1)

Using either the Miner's Arms, or the even older Gate Inn as a base, nearby **Rainster Rocks** above the village has wide open views, a place to enjoy a picnic, or admire the wealth of wild flowers and ferns growing in and around the jagged outcrops.

Kniveton and the hamlet of curiously named **Knockerdown** sit on either side of Hognaston Winn (Winn is an old name version of Ridge). Kniveton shelters in a deep hollow where its grey stone houses and one pub are served by a church whose foundations were laid when the Normans ruled this country. Knockerdown is reputed to be where a battle between the locals and the conquering Roman invaders took place.*(2)

A minor road from Brassington winds through peaceful meadowland to **Bradbourne** where many of the houses date from Tudor times and where the Monks of Dunstable Priory once had a grange farm. The church dates from the 8th century and one can still find a number of crudely carved stones, including the remains of a Saxon cross, within its fabric. Haverhill Dale Brook below the village powered a corn mill beside the B5056 Grangemill to Fenny Bentley road within living memory.

*(2) Archaeological research has led to the theory that the Roman Peak District lead mining headquarters of Lutudaron was on a site now drowned by Carsington reservoir.

North of this road, which here follows the southern boundary of the Peak National Park, and approached by a minor road, **Parwich** sits around a pleasant little village green. **Parwich Hall** though dating from 1747, strangely enough is built of brick, an unusual material in an area where stone came free. Standing on a terrace overlooking the village, the hall gardens are occasionally opened to the public for advertised events. Parwich church though rebuilt in Victorian times, still retains many of its original Norman features.

Narrow lanes wind mostly uphill away from Parwich. **Alsop en le Dale** is, as the name suggests, deep within the confines of a wooded dry dale three miles to the west. Most of its houses are at least 300 years old, but the church, though built on 900 year old foundations, was much altered during the Victorian rebuilding craze. **Ballidon** lies to the east of Parwich where chemically pure limestone is quarried from an adjacent hillside.

Immediately north of Ballidon Quarry and near **Roystone Grange,** lie the remains of a Roman field system, along with traces of a Roman manor house and later medieval buildings. A useful leaflet, obtainable from information centres, and plaques help to guide the way along the Roystone Grange Archaeological Trail starting at Minninglow car park. This is also described in this book. Even older than the Roman fields, **Minninglow** is the dominant tree-covered prehistoric hilltop mound containing a chambered cairn about 1¹/₂ miles to the north east. Although visible over much of the White Peak and close to the High Peak Trail, Minninglow is on private land and can only be visited with permission.

At Gotham to the west of the car park, the High Peak Trail, once a rail link between the Cromford Canal and the High Peak Canal at Whaley Bridge, makes a right angled turn in a 55yd radius, the tightest curve on any standard gauge railway in the world.

Following the trail eastwards brings us to the one time headquarters of lead mining in the south Peak. Now relying on

Parwich, a secluded village in the south of the Peak.

Roystone Grange Walk p 165

St Mary's, Wirksworth's ancient parish church.

limestone quarrying for its staple industry, **Wirksworth** is a town just made for browsing. Narrow jitties (alleys), climb the hillside away from the market place to groups of cottages clustered around tiny yards. So complex is the layout that one part of the hillside is known locally as 'The Puzzle Gardens'.

The Heritage Centre, itself almost hidden in Crown Yard, makes the ideal place to begin to explore Wirksworth. Here you can glean something of the town's history, then using the easy to follow guide, wander round the Town Trail.

The Victorian novelist, Elizabeth Evans writing under her nom-de-plume George Eliot, based her novel Adam Bede in and around Wirksworth, which she called Snowfield.

In Wirksworth: (top left) The Red Lion; (top right) Crown Yard; (middle) B. Payne & Son, one of the oldest chemist shops in the country still dispenses medicines; (above) Barmote Court, Moot Hall.

Restored houses, several dating from Jacobean times, owe their fresh lease of life to the efforts of the local Civic Association, whose 'Wirksworth Project' earned them the accolade of *'brilliantly imaginative '* from HRH Prince Charles. Restaurants, cafés, one-time coaching inns and shops including one of the oldest still-dispensing chemist shops in the country, line streets around the market place. Wirksworth's **Barmote Court** still meets twice a year in the Moot Hall to deal with mining disputes. The public are admitted to this ancient court which sits in April and October on advertised days.

Of all the buildings in Wirksworth, St Mary's, the parish church, is the finest. Cathedral-like it stands behind buildings lining the main street on one side, and the Elizabethan 'Gell Almshouses' and a Georgian former grammar school on the other. Inside the church is the Wirksworth Stone, a stone coffin lid dating from the 8th century, and Wirksworth's unofficial emblem, a carving of a Saxon lead miner, the original *'t'owd man'* of Peakland vernacular. In September, the ceremony of *'Clypping'* the church is performed by parishioners encircling it by holding hands.

Wirksworth wells are dressed at Spring Bank Holiday, and there is also an annual arts and crafts festival in September.

High grade limestone, used mostly in the chemical industry is mined rather than quarried above the town at the hilltop village of **Middleton**. Nearby and just off a side road from Middleton to Black Rocks is the **National Stone Centre**. An independent educational charity, its aim is to tell the story of stone, from its origins and uses, through stone axe factories to modern needs in such diverse industries as sugar refining and steel making. Sited in an old quarry, trails from the centre visit remains of ancient coral reefs and lagoons that once covered the region. Children can pan for gem stones, or make fossil rubbings on a visit which can be part of National Curriculum work. A visit to the Stone Centre could be combined with a look at the **Middleton Top Winding Engine**, especially if it is on one of its steaming days. A narrow gauge railway that once worked from the local quarries, also runs close by on advertised days.

Wirksworth Heritage Centre
Open March to November. Times vary
tel: 01628 825225

Wirksworth Well Dressing, held in May.

National Stone Centre
Open all year.

Castleton, Hope Valley & the Dark Peak

Although limestone dominates much of the south side of the Hope Valley, all the land north of a line drawn roughly along the valley is built on gritstones. The land is mostly acidic, supporting only coarse grasses, heather and on the highest moors, crowberry, a plant found in the arctic tundra regions. This is the Dark Peak, a land of high peaty moorland, a semi-wilderness, the haunt of mountain hare and grouse; an untamed land despite its closeness to the industrial cities of Manchester and Sheffield.

On the eastern edges.

Peveril Castle from Cave Dale, Castleton.

Peveril Castle
Open all year,
Wednesday-Sunday.

Acting like a huge sponge, the moors of the **Dark Peak** are wet and boggy, making walking on them a hazardous expedition still known as 'bog trotting'. Water draining into the high valleys is retained to meet the demands of towns and cities around the Peak District.

Habitation is limited to the lowest valleys surrounding the Dark Peak. Using the local gritstone for building, most of the villages were founded centuries ago. Development within them has been slow and as a result, the villages are mostly compact groups of cottages huddled away from the icy moorland blasts of winter.

Peakshole Water, the main stream along the Hope Valley, flows from a well below Peak Cavern in **Castleton**. The village sits beneath the protection of a castle keep, first erected by William Peveril, one of William the Conqueror's knights. Built to control the local Saxons and also watch over lead mining interests, the castle's only moment of glory was when Henry II accepted the submission of Malcolm, King of Scotland within its walls in 1157. The Victorian novelist Sir Walter

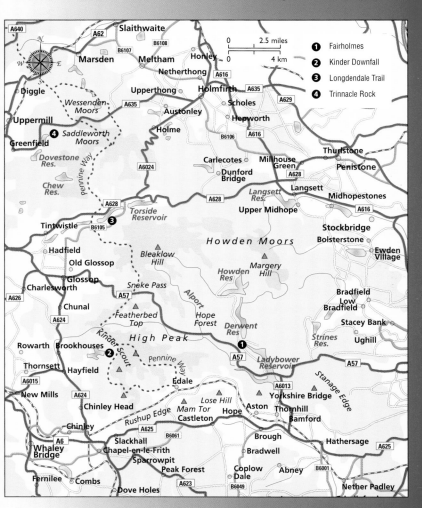

Scott made the castle the over-romantic setting for his *Peveril of the Peak*.

The village is a delightful cluster of stone cottages and interesting inns, all built around the church* founded before the castle was built. The oldest part of the village lies between church and castle, standing mostly to one side of a triangular village green. Shops lining the main street sell semi-precious jewellery, carrying on a tradition

* Inside St Edmund's church is a small 15th century painting of the Adoration of the Magi, attributed to Jan Van Eyck, together with a collection of rare books including a Cranmer Bible of 1539, and a 'Breeches Bible' dating from 1611.

The 'Garland King' heads a procession around Castleton every 29th May.

Castleton Garland Ceremony
Every year on the evening of 29 May, starting from the Peak Hotel car park.

* Pudding in a Lantern

"Tha doesna' know and I duana know
What they ha'; 'Bradda;
An old cow's head on' a piece o' bread,
And a pudding baked in a lantern".

Ollerenshaw Collection of blue john, open all year.

begun when the locally found rarity, blue john stone was more extensively mined than today. During Christmas the shops take on an almost Dickensian look when all Castleton is decorated with illuminated Christmas trees.

Castleton's most famous and unique festivity is the **Garland Ceremony**. Held on Oak Apple Day, a man dressed in Jacobean costume and with his upper body covered by a massive cone of flowers, rides on horseback through the village accompanied by the village band, his lady and dancing children. The band plays a special tune, curiously known as '*Pudding in a Lantern*'*, and pausing at every pub along the way, the procession winds its way to the village green. Here a posy from the top of the 'garland' is placed at the foot of the war memorial and the children dance round a maypole. The main section of the garland is hoisted to the top of one of the church's eight pinnacles, where it is left until it withers. Supposedly commemorating the restoration of King Charles II, the Garland Ceremony probably has its links with ancient Celtic fertility rites.

Three small but interesting collections of local artifacts can be found in Castleton. The National Park Information Centre has a number of old lead mining relics and interpretive stands; the **Ollerenshaw Collection** of blue john ornaments and other semi-precious crystals is opposite the Cheshire Cheese Inn, and the village museum near the main car park has a number of old farming and household implements, gathered from around the area.

Caverns and old lead mines abound in the Castleton area. Most of the public caves were at least partly worked by lead miners, but **Peak Cavern** directly beneath the castle is completely natural, part of an extensive network of underground channels reaching as far as Giant's Hole beneath Rushup Edge to the west. The cave, owned by the Duchy of Cornwall, is open to the public for a considerable distance beyond its imposing entrance. At one time rope makers lived in tiny hovels and had their ropewalks on terraces inside the cave entrance, taking advantage of the constant humidity. Only the terraces and a little of the simple machinery, together with the smoke blackened walls of the cave, remain of an industry whose last worker died within living memory. Demonstrations of ropemaking with this old machinery, are given from time to time.

Attractive cottages line the approach to Peak Cavern (top) and festive Christmas lights decorate Castleton (above).

Peak Cavern
Guided tours of the cavern which has the largest cave entrance in Britain.

Lead mining was once the major occupation of men and frequently women, living in the Hope Valley and Castleton was no exception. Humps and hollows on surrounding hillsides indicate the whereabouts of long abandoned mine workings. These are not places to approach too closely, but a number of both natural caves and part mineworkings are open to the public. The oldest recorded mine, and one which can still be seen if only from its entrance, is **Odin Mine** near the end of the

The Winnats Pass, once part of a tropical lagoon.

Treak Cliff Cavern and **Blue John Cavern**
The only sources of workable blue john. Open all year.

* There has been much conjecture about how Winnats Pass was created. Some geologists favour a collapsed cave system, but the consensus of opinion suggests that the Winnats Pass (or 'Wind Gates'), was once a channel between coral reefs when the Hope Valley was part of a tropical lagoon countless millenia ago.

abandoned section of the A625 above Castleton. As the name suggests this mine was dedicated to the Norse god by early Danish settlers. Worked until the late 18th century, overgrown spoil heaps, together with a partly restored horse-drawn ore crushing ring, can be seen on the opposite side of the road.

The hillside above Odin Mine is known as **Treak Cliff**, where a cavern of the same name contains, along with a fine selection of stalagmites and stalactites, a number of blue john veins. This cave together with its neighbour on the opposite side of the hill, the **Blue John Cavern**, are the only places where this uniquely attractive stone can be found in workable quantities. As the hill is owned by the National Trust, mining blue john is very strictly controlled, and only small amounts are now available for shaping and polishing into jewellery. Some of the finest examples of blue john work are on display in the Ollerenshaw Collection.

Since the A625 was abandoned due to a major land slippage beneath Mam Tor, the only road westwards out of Castleton is along the original 1757 turnpike road climbing steeply up the **Winnats Pass**.* Tall jagged cliffs towering above the road create an awesome driving experience, especially on a winter's night when they become festooned with snow and ice.

Speedwell Cavern at the foot of the Winnats Pass is based on an underground canal cut in 1774 to carry lead ore from deep inside the partly natural mine. Soon uneconomical, mining activity was abandoned, but today's visitors can explore the mine by boat.

In a small museum attached to Speedwell Mine gift shop, a lady's saddle stands as mute reminder of the **Winnats murder** which took place in 1758. At that time due to a quirk of ecclesiastical law it was possible for couples to marry at Peak Forest church without the need for banns. As a result Peak Forest was rather like Gretna Green, where the 'no questions asked' marriages of eloping couples were entered in the register simply as 'Foreign Marriages'.

A star-crossed and richly dressed couple still known only by their Christian names, Clara and Henry, came into Castleton where they were seen by a group of lead miners who followed them into the Winnats Pass. Here they robbed and murdered the couple and threw their bodies down a disused mine shaft. As the couple had successfully evaded pursuit by Clara's parents, no one came to look for them and it was only a day or so later when their ponies were found wandering on the nearby moor, Clara's still bearing her elegant side saddle, that people became concerned. Despite a thorough search, nothing else was found until ten years later when another group of miners stumbled across two skeletons when they broke into an old mine working. Despite a great deal of publicity at the time, no one claimed the remains. It was only by the observant memory of the landlord of the Royal Oak at Stoney Middleton, who recalled Henry having two of his front teeth missing, that the two bodies were at least partially identified.

With the scant knowledge of their names and with the briefest of ceremonies, Clara and Henry were buried in Castleton graveyard. No one was ever charged with the couple's murder, and it was only the deathbed confession of James Ashton, one of the murderers, that threw some light on the tragedy. He would not name his fellow killers, apart from saying they had all died from terrible accidents within the mines. Resting together in an unmarked grave, Clara and Henry's only memorial is the still elegant, bloodstained side saddle.

If the elopers had completed their journey, they would have passed deep Eldon Hole and reached **Peak Forest**, a village which then as now stands mostly away from traffic on the now busy A623, Manchester to Chesterfield road. It was once the headquarters of the High Peak Forest, or *Campagne*, where cruel punishments for infringing hunting laws were enacted. The church where Clara and Henry were hoping to marry was built first as a private chapel within the Royal Forest, by the Countess of Devonshire in 1657. Unusually dedicated to King Charles the Martyr (Charles I), the present building dates from 1877, when it was rebuilt by the 7th Duke of Devonshire.

A minor road south leads towards Miller's Dale and a mile or so out of Peak Forest, a signpost on the right points to Freshfields and the Michael Eliot Trust's Donkey Sanctuary. The charity is supported by the theatrical fraternity, and many well known personalities make regular visits.

The A623 leaves the high ground to meet the A6 outside **Chapel-en-le-Frith.** As the name suggests, the town was originally a foresters' chapel within the Royal Forest of the High Peak. Ferodo brake lining factory employs many of the local residents in an industry begun as a result of the firm's founder watching carters using clogs to improve brakes on their vehicles when descending steep Rushup Edge – hence the term, brake 'shoe'. Despite its industry, much of the town's origins can still be traced around the cobbled market place with its medieval cross and stocks.

Chestnut Centre
Wildlife sanctuary, woodland walks, tea room, gift shop and visitor centre.

Climbing north east towards Rushup Edge, the road passes the **Chestnut Centre** at Slackhall, a conservation centre specialising in owls, otters and other endangered species in 40 acres of woodland and valley.

Edale National Park Information Centre
Near Edale Station. Open all year.

The burial site of an ancient chieftain, **Rushup Edge** and its adjoining neighbour, the Mam Tor to Lose Hill ridge, mark the boundary between limestones of the White Peak in the south and millstone grit based rocks and shales of the Dark Peak to the north. The valley at the northern foot of the three miles of continuous ridge is **Edale**, which, despite its apparent remoteness, has long been used by man. Hamlets and farmsteads in the valley, whose names include the word 'Booth',

indicate they were once simple shelters used only in summer. Where walkers now start their hard climb to the jagged edge of Kinder Scout, packhorse drivers, or *jaggers*,***** stopped for refreshment at the 16th-century Nag's Head Inn.

Edale has a large **National Park Information Centre** where walkers can check local weather conditions as well as learning about the surrounding moors. Two pubs and a café, together with camp sites, B&B, Champion House the Derby Diocese Residential Centre and a YHA Activity Centre complete the range of amenities.

Of the unlimited walking opportunities around Edale the three relatively easy walks described here are just a sample of what is available. One of the walks starts at the foot of **Mam Tor**. Known locally as the 'Shivering Mountain', it is composed mostly of shales on top of clays sitting on the limestone bedrock. As a result of its composition, Mam Tor's southern face is unstable and constantly on the move. By cautiously following the course of the derelict A625 below the Blue John Cavern, it soon becomes apparent why the road was abandoned after years of fruitless repairs. Sections of the road have slumped several feet below their original position on the wet and constantly moving shale.

Nag's Head, Edale, and the start of the Pennine Way.

* Carrying Cheshire salt to Yorkshire and beyond, jaggers entered the Edale valley by way of a winding track, shortened by one of their number called Jacob. His 'ladder', now improved by the National Trust, descends to a narrow bridge used by Pennine Way walkers.

Mam Tor (top) and the
triangulation pillar on
its summit (above).

Bronze Age people built a fort on top of Mam Tor, the outer ditches and some of the hut circles are still visible on the exposed hilltop. A footpath follows the ridge down to Hollins Cross, once a coffin way to Castleton before Edale had its own church. Craggy Back Tor points the way to **Lose Hill**, donated to the National Trust in memory of the late GHB Ward, a Sheffield rambler who did much to gain access to the surrounding moors.

Losehill Hall stands at the foot of its namesake hill, half a mile outside Castleton. Owned and run by the Peak District National Park, it offers residential and day courses and activities, on all matters relating to the national park.

It is known that the village of **Hope***(1) was an important place around the time of the *Domesday Book*, when its parish covered two-thirds of the Royal Forest of High Peak. There is still a small sheep and cattle market which has been held there since its charter in 1715. Opposite the market and the Old Hall Hotel, the church with its stumpy, foreshortened spire, seems to block the road, making it swerve to the north in order to get by. Although most of the present church dates from Victorian times, it does have older foundations dating from the 13th century.

No doubt to control their lead mining interests, the Romans built a fort on the south side of the river near **Brough** below Hope, calling it *Navio*.*(2) Linked to *Aquae Arnemetiae* (modern Buxton), by a road called *Batham Gate* to the south west, a further road also linked the fort to *Ardotalia* near Glossop in the north west. Present day Brough is built around a one-time water mill, now carefully preserved as a farm supplies outlet.

Hidden from the Hope Valley Cement Works by a convenient hill, **Bradwell** sits at the mouth of a north facing narrow limestone dale; an independent village where the links with its lead mining ancestry are evident in the maze of tiny alleys, 'jitties' hereabouts, winding their way up the hillside. Bradwell has long been a place of diverse industry, from its specially designed miners' hats, known as 'Bradder Beavers', to coarse cotton fabrics, opera glasses and the wire umbrella frames invented locally; today the cement works employs the bulk of the working population. Mention must also be

Losehill Hall
Tel: 01433 620373 for details of courses available.

*(1) There has been a village at Hope at least since 926 AD when Saxon King Athelstan won a battle on a nearby hill which has since been called Win Hill. How true this tale is can only be conjectured, especially when linked to Lose Hill where a battle is supposed to have been lost about the same time.

*(2) Legend has it that the garrison at Navio held captive slaves to work in local mines. Nearby Bradwell is supposed to be on the site of a concentration camp where the slaves were housed.

A track leads into the upper Derwent.

Bagshawe Cavern
Two-hour adventure caving trip.
Tel; 01433 620540 for details.

Bamford Sheep Dog Trials
held annually, late May.

Win Hill Walk
p 166

made of the excellent Bradwell's ice-cream made in the village.

Bagshawe Cavern can be found at the head of lanes climbing above the village. Discovered by lead miners in 1806, it is now run as an adventure and training cavern, reached by descending 130 steps.

The A6013 leaves the Hope Valley to follow the main river, the Derwent, upstream towards the Ladybower Reservoir and the A57, Snake Road between Sheffield and Manchester. Before the A6013 reaches Ladybower, it winds through **Bamford**. What was once a water-driven cotton mill and later a factory making electric furnaces, has been converted into an attractive group of waterside flats and apartments. Closely linked to the surrounding hillfarms, Bamford is the venue of the renowned **sheep dog trials** held over the late spring bank holiday weekend. The village is noted for the high standard of food served by its hospitable roadside inns.

A mile or so north from Bamford, a group of stone-built houses stands below the road. This is **Yorkshire Bridge**, built to house the inhabitants of Derwent and Ashopton villages when their homes were flooded by

the waters of the **Ladybower Reservoir**. There is an interesting walk from here to the summit of Win Hill.

Built to provide water for the industrial heartland of the north Midlands, Ladybower was the last of a series of three reservoirs in the upper Derwent. Sometimes called the Peakland Lake District, three dams fill the valley with reservoirs which only the most ardent purist could call unsightly. The first to be built was Howden between 1901 and 1912, rapidly followed by the Derwent, begun in 1902 and finished in 1916.*

When the Ladybower reservoir was built between 1935 and 1943, it drowned two lovely villages, Derwent and Ashopton, where if early photographs are correct, life was idyllic. Among the many buildings sacrificed beneath the waters, were Derwent Hall, dating from 1672, and a property of the Dukes of Norfolk, along with the parish church of St John and St James. Until it was flooded, the hall was used as a youth hostel, one of the first in the Peak District. For a time, the church spire was visible whenever water levels were low, until it was demolished to stop sightseers from endangering themselves in the mud. A narrow bridge which once

Morning mist, Derwent Reservoir.

* To house the army of navvies, or 'navigators', a corrugated iron village was built at Birchinlee, above what became the Derwent Reservoir. Known as 'Tin Town', it housed up to 1,000 men and their families for over 15 years. The village included shops, recreation hall, school, hospital, a canteen in place of a pub and, perhaps because of the latter, a police station. Tin Town was demolished once the work was complete, but the terraces on which it stood and a commemorative plaque, show where it used to be.

(1) Derwent Dam helped Barnes Wallis develop his 'bouncing bomb' during World War 2, and much of the film Dambusters which tells the story of bombing the Ruhr dams, was filmed here.

Fairholmes Visitor Centre, Information, cycle hire, café

Ladybower Walk p 167

Kinder Tresspass Memorial, Bowden Bridge, Hayfield.

(2) A tiny pool below Kinder Downfall is known as the Mermaid's Pool, where anyone visiting the pool on the eve of Easter and seeing the water sprite swimming in it, will be dragged to their doom.

helped packhorses cross the River Derwent, was moved stone by stone to **Slippery Stones** at the head of Howden Reservoir, and now helps walkers to cross dry footed. Carefully managed plantations on both sides of the dale have created a perfect backcloth for the sinuously curving stretches of water.*(1)

Today, the valley has become a useful scenic attraction, a good place to begin a walk, or perhaps hire a bicycle from **Fairholmes Visitor Centre**, and ride round the reservoirs, or simply picnic at one of the amenity sites. Such is its popularity that during summer weekends and bank holidays, traffic is banned from the upper dale, but a regular bus service runs from the car park to King's Tree at the road end. A pleasant walk starts and finishes at Fairholmes car park following first a quiet lane and then paths high above Ladybower, before returning along a pleasant woodland path to the car park.

The A57, Snake road, follows Woodlands Valley beyond the north western arm of Ladybower. Reaching 1680 feet above sea level, it crosses the peaty wastes of Featherbed Moss, the northern outlier of **Kinder Scout**. At 2088 feet, Kinder Scout is the highest point of the Peak District. Not so high when compared with even the Lake District giants, it is however, hardly a place for the foolhardy. Roughly triangular in shape and bounded on all sides by steep gritstone escarpments, a deep boggy plateau fills the interior. So flat is this 'summit', that water channels meander all over the place, cutting through the peat until they either meet bedrock, or at least impervious clay. Known as 'groughs', the maze of channels lies in wait for unwary walkers and it is one of the loneliest parts of England. Strange rock formations carved by centuries of frost and wind create strange visions in the mist. A river taking its name from the hill flows over a steep crag and into a funnel-shaped valley. The waterfall is known as the **Downfall**,*(2) where if the wind is in the right direction, a plume of water visible for miles, is blown high into the air.

A hillside known as Sandy Heys near the Downfall was the scene of the now famous Mass Trespass of 24 April 1932. About 400 ramblers who had set out from Hayfield to bring attention to the need for free access to Kinder Scout, came into confrontation with groups of gamekeepers as they climbed out of the confines of **William Clough**. Scuffles broke out and six ramblers were arrested and later charged with riotous

Top: 'Bog Trotting' across Kinder can be hard work. Above: Mist fills the Edale Valley with cotton wool.

assembly and assault. Five of them received prison sentences of between two and six months at Derby Assizes. Their actions are commemorated by a small plaque above the car park at Bowden Bridge, where the march began. Whether in retrospect their actions were right or wrong, freedom to roam over Kinder is now a right to be enjoyed by all.

Kinder Downfall Walk p167

A walk starting from **Bowden Bridge** near Hayfield, visits the Downfall by way of Sandy Heys and William Clough.

William Clough together with the River Kinder, helps fill Kinder Reservoir. One of the few rights of way tantalisingly available to the intrepid trespassers, followed William Clough to Ashop Head. From here the path runs downhill, following Ashop Clough to join the A57 near the Snake Inn.

Taking its name from the crest of one of its founders, the Duke of Devonshire, the Snake road was opened in 1821 and at 1,680 feet, it was one of the highest turnpike roads in England. The Snake Inn was built about this time, but was originally known as Lady Clough House, where then as now, travellers found warmth and refreshment.

There has been a road over the **Snake Pass** since at least Roman times, linking *Navio* near Brough and *Ardotalia* (frequently, but wrongly called *Melandra*), outside Glossop. Their road followed a slightly higher and more northerly route and can, where it does not coincide with the modern road, be traced along the footpath between Alport Dale and Oyster Clough.

Roman and modern roads over the Snake diverge at Doctor's Gate Culvert. This part of the road takes its name from a Doctor Talbot of Glossop who lived in the early 17th century and is supposed to have restored the old way. Locally the section of the road over the wild moor known as Old Woman and down towards Glossop along Shelf Brook, is known as Doctor's Gate***** ('gate' is an old word for 'way' or 'road').

* *The track immediately north west of Doctor's Gate culvert is one of the best preserved examples of Roman road engineering in the country. About 4 feet 6 inches wide, it is made of flat slabs on either side of a centre stone. Raised kerbstones above a two feet wide ditch mark the outer limits.*

Recently laid paving slabs allow Pennine Way walkers to cross the deep bogs on either side of the Snake Pass. Featherbed Moss to the south of the road sounds gentle and seductive, but more accurate warnings are in the title of Devil's Dike and Hern Stones leading towards **Bleaklow Head**. The Wain Stones mark the highest

point, and when viewed from the correct angle, look like a couple about to kiss! More of a wilderness than even Kinder, **Bleaklow** is one of the last nesting places of the rare black grouse, and where the pure white winter fur of mountain hares acts as camouflage. Orange fruits of the cloudberry hide amongst the less tasty crowberries. In July, sections of the moor turn purple when the heather is in bloom, showing 'Glorious Twelfth' beaters where the red grouse feeds.

Unlike Kinder, the summit of Bleaklow follows a long flat ridge dotted with weather-worn stones; an eerie place where strange lights have been seen. Water draining to the north falls over a line of high crags to fill the reservoirs of **Longdendale**. Once the largest system of man-made lakes in Europe, they were part of Manchester's plan to take pure water into the city and help eradicate disease. Ironically many of those who worked on the dams died from cholera caught in the insanitary conditions of their camps.

A railway once followed Longdendale, tunnelling beneath the Woodhead Pass to reach

Top: Wain Stones, Bleaklow, the "Kiss". Below: Bowden Bridge once echoed the clip-clop of packhorses.

Alport Castles, an ancient landslip.

Dunford Bridge on a northerly route between Manchester and Sheffield. The line is now abandoned and the rails taken away, leaving the track to be used as the **Longdendale Trail**, a traffic-free cycle track. A sailing club uses Torside Reservoir and between it and the trail, a National Park Information Centre makes a useful place to visit before venturing on to the high moors.

Across the reservoir Crowden Youth Hostel and the nearby campsite for lightweight tents make an obvious stopping place for walkers who have just completed the longest and hardest stage of their northerly progression along the Pennine Way. Ahead lie the boggy wastes of Black Hill.* Intrusive electricity pylons marching along the valley of Longdendale, thankfully disappear underground through one of the three abandoned railway tunnels below Woodhead.

* In 1784, surveyors of the Royal Engineers set up one of the first triangulation stations on Black Hill. Their massive teak and brass, 36 inch, Great Ramsden theodolite survives and is on display in the Science Museum, Kensington.

Streams flowing eastwards and south, fill the Derwent dams. Lined with pine trees in its sheltered lower reaches, Alport Dale is dominated by a huge outcrop known as **Alport Castles**. A purely natural phenomenon, the 'castles' are the result of an ancient landslip. At its foot lies Alport Farm, one of the remotest in the Peak District. During the 18th-century religious revivalist movement, it became customary to hold services in remote areas away from the established church. Run as camp meetings and covenanted services, they were frequently linked with 'love feasts', based on the Last Supper. The Woodlands Love Feast carries on this tradition with an annual gathering in a barn at Alport Castles Farm, on the morning of the first Sunday in July.

Free-standing rock outcrops on the long escarpment overlooking the eastern side of the Derwent valley have taken on a wide variety of shapes. Visible landmarks over a wide area, titles such as the Cakes of Bread, or the Salt Cellar, readily describe their shape. One group even looks like a coach and horses battling its way across the moor.

A pattern of winding by-roads links the A57 and A616, Manchester to Sheffield roads. Leaving the A57 at Moscar, the most westerly of these narrow roads winds between the high moors and the tree secluded upper valley of the River Loxley. Remote Strines Inn has given shelter to travellers since the 14th century and below it is **Strines Reservoir** the first of four reservoirs. Today they add to the attractions of the wooded valley, but once caused horrendous flooding when a dam wall collapsed during a cloudburst over a hundred years ago.

High and **Low Bradfield** fit in a sheltering fold of the hillside 860 feet above sea level, aloof from the bustle and industry of Sheffield, a mere 7 miles away. Motte and Bailey fortifications and the Bar Dike, a linear boundary trench on the moors above the village, indicate the venerable ancestry of Bradfield. The church* is Victorian, but stands on the site of a chapel-of-ease built for monks from Ecclesfield Priory in the 14th and 15th centuries. From the church the superb view is enhanced by the boats of Sheffield Sailing Club on Damflask Reservoir.

A cat's cradle of minor roads finds its way across Ewden Beck to **Langsett** where a path around the tree screened 120 acre reservoir makes an easy walk. The village is a sprawl of stone cottages and one pub, lining the A616 where it climbs out of Stocksbridge. None are particularly old, but the aisled barn is. Built in the 17th century, the restored barn now serves as a **National Park Visitor Centre**.

* Close to Bradfield church an oddly shaped private house known as the Watch House, was built in 1745 to guard against body snatchers plundering the adjacent graveyard.

**Langsett Walk
p 167**

Langsett National Park Visitor Centre
Open weekends and Bank Holidays. Easter to end of September.

Sid's Café, Holmfirth
(top) and Nora Batty's
house (above).

Three roads climb the far northern moors and cross the national park boundary to reach two small towns which, although being very much part of the West Riding of Yorkshire, nevertheless are closely linked to the Peak District. The easiest road is the A616 continuing beyond the Flouch Inn, but two others cross the wild moors north of the Woodhead Pass. One is the unclassified road by way of Dunford Bridge and its surprisingly large hotel, a one time shooting lodge. The other is the A6024 climbing steeply out of Longdendale, past the 725ft mast of Holme Moss BBC transmitter before sweeping down to Holmfirth. Passing places are rare on the unremitting climb out of Longdendale, and in icy conditions it is a road to avoid at all costs.

Filming is not new to **Holmfirth**. Nowadays the town is used as a backcloth for episodes of the TV series *Last of the Summer Wine*, but prior to the First World War Holmfirth competed with the then emerging Hollywood as a venue for film making. In 1870 James Bamforth began producing lantern slides which he turned into picture postcards as a sideline. Around 1908 he ventured into the then infant movies, using professional actors, but lack of year-round sunshine and the outbreak of war led to its demise. Ever resourceful, Bamforth concentrated on postcards, especially the comic variety which became the hallmark of the still prosperous Bamforth company. Today's visitors to Holmfirth can follow the footsteps of Compo, Clegg and Foggy, and find settings made familiar through the medium of the TV screen. Sid's Café is alive and flourishing, or you could visit the 'Wrinkled Stocking Tea Room' in Compo's bedroom below Nora Batty's steps. This house is private so please respect the owner's privacy. A *Last of the Summer Wine* Exhibition at Scarfold, off Hollowgate, completes the nostalgic look around Holmfirth.

Last of the Summer Wine **Exhibition** Open daily, all year.

Boasting a thriving artistic community in the surrounding area, there is also a surprisingly large number of galleries displaying works of high standard. On the Sunday before Whitsun, the '**Holmfirth Sing**' is held in Victoria Park, or in the church if it rains. This unique event which began in 1882, allows everyone to join in singing excerpts from the *Messiah*, and other choral works. **Harden Moss Sheepdog Trials** are held on the moors above the A623 road outside Holmfirth.

Harden Moss Sheepdog Trials, held over two days in June.

Crossing the bleak wastes of Wessenden Head and notorious Saddleworth Moors, the A635 descends into Lancashire. Here the stone cottages of one-time textile workers in villages like Uppermill and Greenfield have taken on a fresh lease of life as dwellings for Manchester commuters. This is the home of brass bands and Lancashire League cricket where matches are hotly contested. It is from here that first-class players are bred to take part in annual re-enactments of the Wars of the Roses against the other side of the Pennines.

Binn Green Walk
p 167

Dropping towards Greenfield, the A635 passes Binn Green car park and picnic site above Yeoman Hey Reservoir, and the start of a challenging walk. Above the reservoir, the route follows a rocky escarpment highlighted by the spectacular **Trinnacle Rock** near Raven Stones. Finding its way south, the walk turns at Chew reservoir; built in 1912, it is the highest constructed reservoir in England.

The national park boundary follows a zig-zag line south of the Saddleworth Moors, to **Tintwistle**, a village that grew from a few handloom weavers' cottages to its present size in the early 19th century with the expansion of King Cotton, and then across Longdendale to make a tight curve around Glossop.

* Away from the main areas of work, employees in the local mills were forbidden to join unions long after it became the norm in more enlightened factories. Resorting to subterfuge, early branches of textile unions met in secret without any member officially acknowledging the names of his colleagues.

Glossop is in two parts, Old Glossop and Howardstown, built by the Duke of Norfolk around Norfolk Square, as an industrial enclave for the Lancashire textile industry.***** With the exception of print works on the outskirts of the town, all the mills are used for industries divorced from textiles. Houses once semi-derelict are now restored and the town has an air of quiet prosperity. To find more about Glossop, visit the **Heritage Centre** in Henry Street, or the Tourist Information Centre on the railway station forecourt.

Glossop Heritage
Centre
History, exhibitions, art gallery. Open all year.

South of Glossop, the A624 climbs steadily, past the Grouse Inn where a minor road to the right climbs further to skirt Cown Edge. This is the Monks' Road, named after the monks of Basingwerk Abbey in Flintshire, who owned the land around here until the Dissolution. Two upright stones below the edge, known as Robin Hood's Picking Rods, are thought to mark the abbey's northern boundary.

Cown Edge is a shaley escarpment overlooking the Etherow Valley and Werneth Low, part of Greater Manchester's countryside. To the south of the escarpment, lies the village of **Rowarth** with its secluded yet popular Little Mill Inn complete with the *Derbyshire Belle*, a Pullman restaurant car converted into bed and breakfast accommodation.

Moving south east across Lantern Pike, **Hayfield** sits comfortably away from traffic hurrying along its by-pass. As its river, the Sett, is west flowing, the village is strictly part of Chapter 5 but as Hayfield has always been linked to Kinder, it is more logical to include it here. A starting point for walks on Kinder Scout and the surrounding moors, Hayfield has always welcomed visitors, be they the leaders of packhorse trains, or modern fell walkers, and the old fashioned inns offer warm hospitality. There are many pleasant walks starting from Hayfield and a short and easy cycle trail, ideal for beginners and known as the **Sett Valley Trail**, follows part of the old railway line between Hayfield and New Mills.

Lantern Pike Walk p 168

Middle Moor and Little Hayfield Walk p 168

The Western Dales

With the exception of the River Churnet and its tributaries, all the valleys and dales on the west side of the Peak flow into the Irish Sea via the Mersey basin. All start their lives amidst heather-clad moors, the haunt of sheep and red grouse. Leaving these heights every river, to a greater or lesser degree, has served the needs of man since the time of the Industrial Revolution. Once heavily polluted in their lower reaches, they have in recent years, regained their early beauty; each valley, the Goyt, Etherow, Bollin, Dane and Churnet, offers a diversity of activities ranging from fishing, sailing and rock climbing to easy walking, or just admiring the view.

Lyme Hall.

The Shrine, Errwood, Goyt Valley.

Starting its life in the western arm of the Peak above Buxton, the Goyt flows roughly northwards before being joined by the Etherow below Marple. Here the river turns to the west to join the Tame at Stockport and the start of the Mersey.

Draining heather moors surrounding the Cat and Fiddle Inn, the second highest public house in Britain, the Goyt below Derbyshire Bridge flows through a deep wooded ravine. Even though there is a road along the valley, it is one way only, and also closed to traffic at weekends and bank holidays. Two reservoirs flood the middle reaches of the **Goyt valley**, Errwood and Fernilee, with a sailing club using the former.

Long before **Errwood Reservoir** was built in 1967, a self-supporting estate existed in and around Errwood Hall, home of the Grimshawe family. Abandoned in 1930, all that remains are the sombre ruins, together with rhododendrons and mature specimen trees surrounding the hall. The reservoir also covers the original site of a packhorse bridge* that crossed the Goyt a little below the hall.

* Moved stone by stone and rebuilt, Goyt Bridge now spans the river a mile upstream of the reservoir, and close to an attractive picnic site.

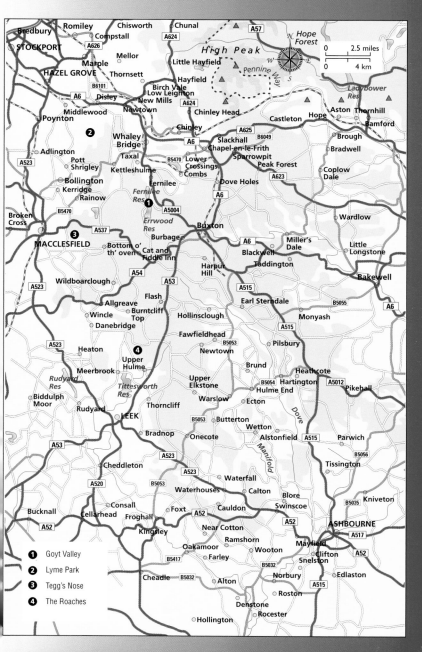

Shining Tor and Errwood Hall Walk p 168

A Catholic family, the Grimshawes employed a Spanish governess to educate their children. She died while living at Errwood and the family built a beautiful chapel in her memory. To reach the well-looked-after tiny circular shrine, follow the walk which explores established woodland above the reservoir, combined with a high level ramble along the ridge leading to **Shining Tor**. On a clear day the view from the tor not only encompasses the high moors of the Dark Peak to the east, but also the Cheshire Plain and the Welsh Mountains in the west.

The Cromford and High Peak Railway made its penultimate descent by dropping into the Goyt Valley, down an incline now used by the access road from Long Hill to Bunsal Cob. The abandoned track bed, level beyond the top of the incline, is accessible to wheelchairs, making it possible for disabled people to reach far into the moors.

Fernilee Walk p 169

Fernilee Reservoir dates from 1938 and mixed forest planted at that time has now matured, making an attractive scene when viewed from the A5002, Long Hill road. A circular walk round the reservoir passes this viewpoint.

The valley is still deeply cut and wooded below Fernilee. Straddling the national park boundary, **Taxal** looks very much as it did three centuries ago when most of its gritstone houses were built. Despite the difference in size, Taxal is senior to its neighbour, Whaley Bridge and its church serves as parish church for the two places.

A glimpse of Taxal in the Goyt Valley.

The remote and secluded side valley of **Todd Brook** starts its life below Shining Tor. A road from the dam separating Errwood and Fernilee reservoirs, climbs to Oldgate Nick where a right turn descends past Windgather Rocks, training ground for countless Peakland rock climbers. The other road was originally made for packhorses bearing loads of salt and drops steeply into Cheshire to cross Todd Brook by the old Saltersford. Jenkin Chapel

stands high above a bridge erected to ease the river crossing. Built in 1733, it has house-sized windows and a chimney, which despite a saddleback tower added in 1755, give it a cosily domestic look. Inside are the original box pews, pulpit and a reading desk. Open-air harvest festivals are held in September.

The B5470 from Whaley Bridge to Macclesfield, passes through tiny **Kettleshulme** where narrow alleys and lanes once echoed to the tramp of clogs worn by operatives of candlewick mills in the valley bottom. One of these mills which ceased work in 1937 still stands at the end of a narrow side lane. Whitewashed Bow Stones Farm* marks the north eastern skyline.

Todd Brook is dammed below Kettleshulme, its water used to fill Peak Forest Canal at its **Whaley Bridge** terminus. Over the couple of centuries since it was built, the reservoir has become an attractive place to sail, and being naturally stocked with fish, gives good prospects for anglers. A modern bleach works at **Horwich End** is all that is left of Whaley Bridge's once thriving textile mills. The Cromford and High Peak Railway descended an incline ending at the canal basin, where a restored warehouse marks the end of the line and the beginning of the canal. Nowadays colourful barges and pleasure craft pause before beginning the long winding cruise into the Cheshire Ring canal network.

Whaley Bridge, the start of the High Peak Canal.

* Visible for miles, Bow Stones farm is named after two strange upright columns of rock. Even though they may, as the name suggests, have been used for bending or stringing bows, the stones were more likely to have been erected to mark the northern boundary of Macclesfield Forest.

About a mile north of Whaley Bridge, a short branch of the canal leads to Bugsworth Basin. By popular demand the nearby village is known as **Buxworth**, and is linked with Whaley Bridge by a side road past the enigmatic *Roosdyche*. Once thought to be a Roman arena, geologists now suggest it is more likely to be a landslip. **Bugsworth Basin** which is gradually being restored to its former glory was once the terminus of a tramway built in 1800 by Benjamin Outram to carry limestone from Dove Holes. Parts of this gravity-operated tramway can still be seen, including stone ties, or sleepers beside a rough track following the tramway south of Chinley.

Chinley came into being as a railway village, but today relies on nearby chemical and textile works for employment. Above it is the mass of Chinley Churn, and the twin peaks of South Head and Mount Famine which provide some very enjoyable walking.

Chinley Churn Walk p 169

South Head Walk p 169

The elongated cone of Eccles Pike overlooks Chapel-en-le-Frith (see chapter 4), and the grouse moor of Combs Moss. This moorland outlier of the Dark Peak once protected an ancient tribe who built a small earthwork above the popular crag of Castle Naze. The village of Combs sits at the foot of the moor, a cluster of old and modern houses together with an excellent pub, blending well into the landscape. The nearby reservoir still provides Peak Forest Canal with water and also offers sport for anglers and members of the local sailing club. An easy walk around Combs gives views over the reservoir.

Combs Walk p169

A waymarked route, the **Goyt Way** along the Goyt Valley, starts by following the Peak Forest Canal from Whaley Bridge, then descends to the valley and into an almost hidden gorge far beneath New Mills. Reaching Marple, the short trail (it can be followed easily in a day's walk) climbs back to the canal and then descends a long flight of locks above Brabyns Park and the end of the walk.

New Mills hides its best features in a rocky gorge deep below the town centre. The town grew from a scattered group of hamlets using the power of both the Sett and Goyt to drive cotton mills. A heritage centre behind the shops tells the story of the town's development. From it a cobbled lane drops steeply into a tree-lined gorge called the Torrs, with the romantic ruins of long abandoned mills set above the powerful river.

New Mills Heritage Centre
Simulated coal mine, model of town in 1884. Open all year Tuesday-Sunday plus Bank Holidays.

The valley beyond New Mills is still partly industrial, but full of interesting nooks and crannies. Only the ruins of the early Industrial Revolution cotton mills built by partnerships of Samuel Oldknow and Richard Arkwright near Marple remain. Man made water courses, known fancifully as Roman Lakes, are stocked with huge fish awaiting the attentions of local anglers; (fees are payable and keep nets are not allowed). A packhorse bridge across the Goyt upstream of the ponds, is also erroneously attributed to Roman builders.

High above the valley, **Marple's** archaeological attractions are built around its canal system. Once the busy junction of the Peak Forest and Macclesfield canals, sensitively renovated warehouses line the canal bank, together with a

cleverly designed set of lime kilns where stone carried on the Peak Forest Canal was tipped into the tops of the kilns. After burning, the resulting lime fell by gravity into barges waiting on a lower arm of the canal. A long flight of locks carries the canal down to an aqueduct crossing the lower Goyt. The river is joined here by the Etherow, a river draining the high moors of Woodhead and Longdendale.

Etherow Country Park follows the valley above **Compstall**, a once industrial village on the B6104 Marple to Romiley road. Well maintained woodland paths follow a series of reservoirs and water courses that once fed a print works. Stocked with fish, the ponds are a popular venue for anglers. There is also a section devoted to radio controlled model boating

Top: The Torrs, hidden industrial history beneath New Mills.
Above: the Macclesfield and Peak Forest canals join at Marple.

Lyme Hall's sheltered Dutch garden is filled with tulips in spring.

Lyme Park
House and gardens open April to October. Country park open daily all year. Children's playground and coffee shop.

* Lyme was used in the recent TV adaptation of Jane Austen's Pride and Prejudice *when it appeared as 'Pemberley', home of the dashing Mr Darcy.*

enthusiasts. Look out for giant terrapins sunning themselves nearby. Like the Roaches wallabies, they are the descendants of abandoned pets which have managed to attune themselves to our climate. In this case they survive by hibernating in mud on the bottom of the pond.

Beyond Disley, the A6 passes the entrance to **Lyme Park**. Set amongst several hundred acres of deer park, woodlands and moors, Lyme was the home of the Legh family for over 600 years. Originally a Tudor house, it was transformed by the Venetian architect Leoni into an Italianate palace, one of the grandest buildings in Cheshire. Parts of the Elizabethan interior survive, contrasting dramatically with later rooms. Mortlake tapestries, Grinling Gibbon wood carvings and an important collection of English clocks decorate the main rooms. Outside, a sunken Dutch garden, rose gardens and a great conservatory all set above an attractive lake, make a pleasing foreground to the medieval deer park.*

As the approach to the hall hides it almost until the last moment, Lyme's more visible attraction is the hunting tower, or 'Cage' standing on top of a low ridge overlooking the hall. From it the view takes in the whole of Greater Manchester, the Cheshire Plain and the foothills of Snowdonia.

A long distance path, the **Gritstone Trail** from Lyme Hall to Rudyard Lake in North Staffordshire leads south past Bow Stones Farm and across Sponds Hill. A walk from Lyme follows part of the trail before returning to the park.

Pott Shrigley nestles in a south facing wooded hollow below Lyme Park. It stands at the junction of a minor road from Poynton and the moorland road from Kettleshulme to Bollington. A simple cluster of stone cottages, its church dates from the 15th century and nearby, the one-time catholic seminary is now a country club and hotel. Even though the village is small, it manages to support a cricket team who use the ever so slightly tilted field beyond the church. Nab Head to the south-west overlooks the Cheshire Plain, and makes an excellent vantage point, especially on summer evenings.

Initially two minor streams drain the mid-western boundary of the Peak National Park. The Dean's headwaters are temporarily held back by **Lamaload Reservoir**, whose sheltered banks are ideal for fishing or picnicking.*

Anyone following the Gritstone Trail has to pass through **Bollington**, a jumble of interesting old gritstone cottages within the confines of a narrow gap between Nab Head and Kerridge Hill. Here the trail climbs exhaustingly to the White Nancy, a curious whitewashed pear-shaped cairn above the town. As an easier alternative, the Middlewood Trail using the old railway line from Bollington, can, when linked to the almost parallel canal, make a safe traffic-free cycle tour.

Macclesfield being the main town for communities along the mid-western boundary of the Peak, is a good shopping centre with many other amenities. Once a silk making town, its origins as a market town are even older. The last silk mill closed in 1981, but the links the town had with the trade are preserved in **Paradise Mill**, a working silk weaving mill. Macclesfield's **Heritage Centre** in Roe Street is also worth visiting. St Michael's Church, though largely rebuilt, has a number of medieval effigies in the Legh and Savage chapels.

Lyme Park, Bow Stones and Sponds Hill Walk p 170

*Above Lamaload Reservoir on the back road to Rainow, a memorial tells of the demise of John Turner during a severe blizzard in 1755. The stone's reverse hints of a mystery when it speaks of the imprint of a woman's shoe being seen near his body, but gives no further explanation.

Paradise Mill
Living museum demonstrating process of silk production.

Macclesfield Heritage Centre, includes the Silk Museum. History of the town and the silk industry.

Gawsworth Hall
Unique Elizabethan gardens and parkland. Open April to October.

Gawsworth Hall lies to the south west of Macclesfield, away from the A536. The lovely half-timbered 15th-century house with later additions, though private, is open to the public. In the 17th-century estate church, monuments to the Fittons include one to Mary Fitton (she died in about 1620) who was reputed to be the 'Dark Lady' of Shakespeare's sonnets.

Tegg's Nose Country Park
Waymarked trails, orienteering course, visitor centre.

The A537 Buxton road climbs steeply out of Macclesfield to Walker Barn where by the Setter Dog Inn, is a side road leading to **Tegg's Nose Country Park**. Based on an old sandstone quarry high above the Cheshire Plain, the park offers everything from short walks to abseiling and rock climbing with qualified instructors. Restored quarry machinery and interpretive plaques help to explain the hard working conditions of quarrymen at Tegg's Nose Quarry. The quarry takes its name from a nearby hilltop, home of a mythical giant called Tegga.

**Tegg's Nose Walk
p170**

While the Gritstone Trail continues south by way of Tegg's Nose, it is possible to take a shorter walk from the car park, across the valley and through Macclesfield Forest.

Beyond Tegg's Nose dense ranks of mature pines in **Macclesfield Forest** line the River Bollin's highest side valleys. Dominated by the symmetrical cone of Shutlingsloe, the view continues south along a series of ridges culminating in the rocky escarpment of the Roaches. Four small reservoirs fit neatly into the valley bottom, popular breeding grounds for water fowl, including such rarities as crested grebe, and migrating birds of passage. Badgers live in secluded setts, while shy roe deer have been seen flitting across sunlit glades.

**Macclesfield Forest and Shutlingsloe Walk
p 170**

The three lower reservoirs, Teggsnose, Bottoms and Ridgegate are available for fishing by permit only. Trentabank, the upper reservoir, is the preserve of wildfowl which with the help of interpretive plaques, can be viewed from an adjacent car park. The car park is also the start of a walk over Shutlingsloe and down into Wildboarclough before returning via Piggford Moor and paths to the south of Macclesfield Forest. The effort involved in this walk is rewarded by the fact that it passes two hospitable pubs along the way, the Crag Inn and the Hanging Gate.

A minor road above Langley passes Leather's Smithy Inn and its renowned catering, before climbing steeply through the forest and over the ancient, now enclosed by trees, vantage point of Toot Hill. On the downward slope the hamlet of **Macclesfield Forest*** (1) dates from the time when the surrounding countryside was part of the medieval chase, not as now, a plantation.

Three Shires Bridge, Dane Valley.

It is a long time since wild boar roamed in **Wildboarclough.** The last one is said to have been killed in the 15th century, but the valley, a tributary of the **River Dane**, has seen little major development since then. Curiously named **Bottom-of-the-Oven**, a group of scattered farms and a pub sit around a road junction below the valley head. Downstream, the valley has recovered from a disastrous flood caused by a spectacular cloudburst a decade or so ago, and now wanders gently along, over slabby waterfalls and through woods where the only sound is birdsong. An estate village serving Lord Derby's Crag Hall, Wildboarclough once boasted the largest sub-post office in England; it was in the old silk mill below the church, but is now a private house.

*(1) On the nearest Sunday to the 12th August the tiny chapel at Macclesfield Forest holds a rush-bearing ceremony. Originally a way of keeping the floor clean, and once a common practice in the Peak, this is one of the few places where the custom continues.

The scant ruins of a paper mill at **Allgreave** stand above the junction of Clough Brook and the River Dane. Born within half a mile of the Goyt on the boggy moors below the Cat and Fiddle, the Dane flows through upland pastures to the point where Cheshire, Staffordshire and Derbyshire all meet. The stream below **Three Shires Head** is crossed by a narrow stone arched bridge that once carried packhorse traffic, and Panniers Pool beneath the bridge got its name as the watering place for pack animals. A walk from Flash includes a visit to this old bridge.

Three Shires Head Walk p 170

Flash is the highest village in England. Standing well back from the A53 Leek to Buxton road, it is served by a minor road into the Dane Valley; a place where winter starts early and lingers long after spring arrives in more sheltered places.*(2)

*(2) Flash once had the reputation of harbouring counterfeiters. Now a much more law abiding place, the only link with that rough and ready time, is the expression 'flashy' for anything suspicious, or fake.

Tiny farmsteads dot the moors. Now mostly private houses, their grazing amalgamated into larger and more economical holdings, the farms never did more than support a sparse living. Running the farms on a part-time basis, their owners found extra employment in local mills, or from mining coal beneath the bleak moors. One can forgive the short lived joy of coal miners who thought they had found gold, but it was 'fool's gold', iron pyrites. Traces of this attractive stone can still be found in stream beds below the aptly named Goldsitch Moss.

One of the last mills to operate in the Dane Valley was at **Gradbach**. The former 18th-century silk mill, built on the site of an earlier structure that burned down in 1785, and later became a saw mill for the Harpur Crewe Estates, has been sensitively restored and now finds a modern use as a youth hostel.

To the west of Gradbach, a woodland track leads to the strange 20ft wide rocky cleft known as **Lud's Church** on the upper limits of Back Forest. In the 14th century it was the secret meeting place of John Wyclif's Lollards, dissenters who objected to the wealth and power of the established church; but the strange ravine has a much older history.*

The title 'Lud' comes from from the name of Walter de Lud-Auk, and is linked to the medieval poem Sir Gawain and the Green Knight. *Modern research suggests that Lud's Church was the Green Chapel mentioned in the poem, and nearby Swythamley Hall is built on the site of the Green Knight's castle.*

Danebridge Walk p 171

Although their numbers are rapidly in decline, red necked wallabies are occasionally seen browsing amongst the heather. These unexpected marsupials are the descendants of a group of animals released to fend for themselves during the austere early days of World War 2. They, together with a pair of llamas and a yak, were part of a private zoo on the Roaches owned by the Brocklehurst family who then lived at **Swythamley Hall**. The hall is private, but plaques on the isolated Hanging Stone give a hint of the Brocklehursts' life. Hanging Stone projects from the hillside and the plaques can be seen while on the walk from Danebridge to Gradbach. One is to a pet family dog and the other commemorates Lieutenant Colonel Brocklehurst, a game warden in the Sudan, and who established the private zoo.

Having amalgamated with the waters of Clough Brook, the Dane is a fair-sized stream by the time it flows under **Danebridge.** The attractive hamlet takes its name from the bridge and once supported one of

Rockhall, the Roaches.

the Dane Valley mills. It has one inn, the Ship***** where one of Bonnie Prince Charlie's soldiers abandoned his flintlock gun during his flight back to Scotland in 1745.

Climbing steeply, the road reaches **Wincle** where the church and a handful of gritstone houses, all with attractive gardens, are all that is left of a once larger village. The by-road continues to climb until it joins the A54 Buxton to Congleton road near Cleulow Cross on the side of Wincle Minn ridge. This once important waymark cross is now hidden within a small plantation.

* The sign of the Ship Inn represents the SS Nimrod in which Sir Philip Brocklehurst sailed to the Antarctic with the explorer Sir Ernest Shackleton in 1909.

Part in and part out of the national park boundary, the far south western corner of the Peak District comprising the Staffordshire Moorlands and the Churnet Valley, is comparatively little known. A wedge of high gritstone rocks marks the highest point, from which all streams flow to join the Churnet. This is an area of contrasts, from the wild moors of Morridge and the Roaches, to Alton Towers where, despite the thousands who flock there each year, the tranquillity of the nearby Churnet Valley remains undisturbed.

The name **Roaches** is the anglicized version of the French *'rocher'*, or simply 'rocks', given to the dramatic escarpment by the monks of Dieulacress Abbey near

Leek. It is very much the preserve of climbers who tackle some of the hardest and certainly longest, gritstone climbs in the Peak. One of the climbs is known as *The Sloth* from the amount of time spent hanging upside down! A quaint cottage known as Rockhall,* formerly a gamekeeper's lodge, is now a climbers' hut in memory of the late Mancunian mountaineer, Don Whillans.

* At one time Rockhall was the abode of a colourful eccentric known as the Lord of the Roaches, who along with his wife, waged an unceasing battle with climbers and walkers.

The Roaches Walk p 171

In 1975 the 975 acre Roaches Estate was bought by the Peak Park Board, making it possible to enjoy the rocks and nearby Hen Cloud without hindrance. A figure of eight walk crosses the skyline and explores the nearby moors. One of the features above the escarpment is Doxey Pool said to be the haunt of a mermaid.

Forming a south facing 'V', the escarpment has sharp pointed Hen Cloud at its apex, then an intermittent line of crags, starting with **Ramshaw Rocks**, towers above the A53 Leek to Buxton road, almost as far as Flash. To the east of the road the stark warning in red on the OS map of DANGER AREA, warns of a military training area. On the opposite side of the road, a projecting rock known as the Winking Man, lives up to its name as you motor towards Leek.

Tittesworth Reservoir
Visitor centre, bird hide, scented garden, café, fishing.

Meerbrook village was scheduled to be demolished when the water company extended **Tittesworth Reservoir**. Fortunately there was a change of heart and the tiny village has returned to its former condition with anglers, bird watchers, walkers, cyclists and motorists enjoying the hospitality of the Lazy Trout public house. The reservoir is stocked with a good range of fish not only enjoyed by anglers, but occasionally by ospreys. These magnificent birds of prey have been seen stocking up for their long migration flight south.

A park and ride scheme operates on summer weekends and Bank Holidays between Tittesworth Reservoir and the Roaches.

Until they were banished during the Dissolution of the Monasteries by Henry VIII in 1538, Cistercian monks lived a comfortable life at Dieulacress Abbey. Little remains of the once grand monastery, which in any case is on private land between Tittesworth and Leek. The only hint of its whereabouts is in the name of Abbey Farm and the adjacent inn.

Part textile town and part market, **Leek** has much on offer to the visitor. The church was old at the time of the Conquest and should be visited, if only to admire the beautiful rose window; or maybe smile at the ducking stool, or puzzle over a grave near the west door which suggests its occupant lived to be over 400 years old. The town's old cobbled market street is almost opposite the church and around it can be found

Rudyard Lake.

a wide range of factory shops together with quaint pubs and welcoming cafés. A leisure centre and museum, library and art school housed in the 17th-century Greystones mansion complete the town's central features. Leek mills mainly produced silk, but today the town specialises in dyeing and finishing textiles.*(1)

James Brindley, the canal engineer and millwright built a **water powered corn mill** next to the Macclesfield road in the lower part of the town. With its restored water wheels and old grinding machinery, the mill is open to visitors at weekends and Bank Holidays throughout the summer.

About three miles to the north of Leek and a half mile west of the A523, Macclesfield road, is the Victorian lakeside resort of **Rudyard***(2); the 'lake' is a reservoir built in 1799 to feed the Caldon Canal. A popular venue for fishing and sailing – a public slipway is sited near the dam – the wooded banks of **Rudyard Lake** make an ideal picnic spot. Sections of the old North Staffordshire Railway which ran along the east bank of the lake, are used first as a lakeside footpath, then for a miniature railway, and finally as a nature reserve.

Rushton Spencer is a little to the north of the lake, where trains once stopped at the magnificent Gothic station, now a private house. Its church which serves a scattered community, stands on a nearby hilltop. Built in an appealing mixture of styles, it is known locally as 'The Chapel in the Wilderness'.

*(1) At Leek a School of Needlework founded by Elizabeth - later Lady Wardle - around 1870, together with the Leek Embroidery Society, produced work of a very high standard. One of the early works of the society is a copy of the Bayeux Tapestry, which strangely found its way to Reading Museum.

Brindley Mill, Leek
Restored mill houses a museum dedicated to James Brindley.

*(2) The parents of the novelist and journalist Rudyard Kipling became engaged at Rudyard and named their son after it.

Opportunities for walking in the Staffordshire Moorlands abound. Rushton Spencer sees the linking of the Gritstone Trail which has come south from Lyme Park, to the Staffordshire Way. This long distance 95 mile trail winds its way along the Churnet Valley to Uttoxeter, then across Cannock Chase to Kinver Edge in the south of the county.

**Rudyard Lake Walk
p 171**

Linked paths, part of the Staffordshire Moorlands Walks, can be followed either as a 4 mile walk around Rudyard Lake, or for the more adventurous, above and along the **Churnet Valley**. Once called 'The Lost Valley', the Churnet is one of the least known valleys around the Peak District. Rich in flora and fauna, its name means the 'river of many windings', and is canalised between Leek and Cheddleton. This arm of the Caldon Canal still links the valley to the Potteries.

Flint Mill, Cheddleton
Working exhibitions of processing of materials for the pottery industry. Open all year.

Churnet Valley Railway
Cheddleton Station. Nostalgic steam train rides.

In the oldest part of **Cheddleton**, the Churnet still drives two waterwheels of a **flint-crushing mill**, once making the strengthening additive for china clay. Originating in 1694, it was restored by a trust in 1969. Cheddleton still has its old stocks, standing below the church wall opposite the Black Lion Inn.

Although the railway line that once linked Leek to Uttoxeter now only runs as far as Oakamoor, it still carries freight in the form of high grade silica sand, but more important to visitors, passenger trains also operate. Frequently hauled by steam locomotives they run from the **Staffordshire Railway Centre** in Cheddleton's ornate Victorian station.

**Combes Valley Walk
p 171**

Combes Valley Nature Reserve
Wooded area, rich in bird life. Bird hides, small visitor centre.

Combes Valley Nature Reserve is reached by a minor road between Cheddleton and the Leek to Ashbourne road. Only two paths cross the deeply cut valley, but they can be linked by way of the privately owned Jacobean Sharpcliffe Hall. Spirit Holes Wood in the valley bottom is said to be the haunt of the devil, and in the riverbed near an overgrown quarry, a huge stone is known as the Giant Osler's Stone. It is supposed to cover a giant who terrified the locals in times gone by.

With one or two minor exceptions in its lower reaches, there are no roads along the Churnet Valley; only the canal and railway offer the means of travel. Despite the lack of roads, industry flourished along this valley, some of it still operating. River and canal are one as far as **Consall Forge**. The only other way into Consall Forge is by the private road used to carry supplies to the Black Lion, a canalside inn opposite a line of abandoned kilns. Another way to reach the pub is down a long flight of steps known as The Devil's Staircase, about two miles west of Ipstones.

Canal and river part company at the weir below Consall Forge, with the canal continuing to **Froghall.** Here A.S. Bolton's copper works began in 1890, turning Ecton copper into wire. The line of a tramway built in 1777 runs uphill to Cauldon Low, where the landlord of the Yew Tree has filled the bar with all manner of antiques, especially old musical instruments, and a pair of Queen Victoria's black silk stockings! The canal now ends at Froghall by an attractive wharf and picnic site where horse drawn narrow boats ply in summer. **Oakamoor** is served only by the B5417 Cauldon Low to Cheadle road and two very minor side roads. There are two nice pubs in Oakamoor and a picnic site within the foundations of an abandoned copper works, where wire was made for the first trans-Atlantic telegraph cable in 1856.

Above a secluded dell at Cotton north east of Oakamoor and reached along a side lane leaving the B5417 at the Old Star Inn, the Roman Catholic seminary has trained priests and missionaries for over a century

Following the road in the direction of Cheadle, it climbs past the nature reserve of **Hawksmoor Wood** and after a mile, passes, on the left, the yard of a Les Oakes and Sons, Hales View Farm. While the main business is that of general merchant, the greatest interest lies in the huge and sometimes eccentric, collection of antique farm implements, horse drawn vehicles and other artifacts. Although the yard is open most days, the private collection can only be viewed by prior arrangement – Tel: (01538) 752126.

Les Oakes' eccentric builder's yard.

Pugin's Rhineland castle; Alton in the Churnet Valley.

An exhilarating ride at Alton Towers.

Below Oakamoor the Churnet enters what is arguably its most attractive zone. This is the area around **Dimmingsdale**, a beech wood surrounding a series of narrow ponds that once powered the bellows of a smelting mill. Here is woodland made for wandering, along footpaths that seem to start anywhere and go somewhere. At the end of an hour or two's stroll how better to end it than at the **Rambler's Retreat Coffee House** at the roadside.

One of the paths climbs by way of the ancient vantage point at Toot Hill to reach **Alton.** The village was once owned by the Earls of Shrewsbury who lived opposite at Alton Towers. Alton Castle overlooks the village and was built to look like a Rhineland castle by the Victorian architect A.W. Pugin who also designed the Gothic Alton Towers for the 15th Earl. Built on the site of Bertram de Verdun's 12th-century fortification, the present castle has had a chequered career as no one seems to stay there very long. The village warrants more than a cursory glance, if only to enjoy a meal at the comfortable Wild Duck Inn, or admire the sturdy circular stone village 'lock-up'.

Alton Towers, is the place to go for stomach-tingling, self-inflicted terror. Here almost yearly yet more terrifying rides are built, with the latest costing £12 million to carry its passengers high into the air, then drop vertically into a completely dark tunnel. The 120 plus rides and other attractions, are set in the grounds of the partial ruins of a large Gothic country house surrounded by extensive gardens. Rhododendrons and water gardens set off against the Chinese Pagoda fountain have now been restored to their former glory, and make a visit to Alton Towers a must even for those with no desire to be thrown at unimaginable speeds around some death-defying ride.

Alton Towers
Theme park and gardens.
Open March to
November.

The river continues south past **Denstone** and its college to mingle with the Dove at **Rocester**. This is the site of **J.C. Bamford's main factory**. Begun in a small way after World War 2, JCB now make the world renowned range of excavators in premises that fit cleverly into the landscape. Ponds dug no doubt with JCB equipment, attract a wide range of aquatic birds, and sculptures, some whimsically made from discarded excavator buckets, catch the eye. A yachting centre and a 26-acre leisure park provided by the firm, are also available nearby.

At Rocester the valleys of both the Churnet and Dove, having lost their hilly nature, make a logical conclusion to this guide to the Peak District.

Monsal Dale walk
Chapter 1 page 158

Sheepwash Bridge, Ashford Lake walk
Chapter 1 page 158

Market Hall, Winster walk
Chapter 2 page 162

Cromford and Black Rocks walk
Chapter 2 page 163

Viator's Bridge walk
Chapter 3 page 164

Kinder Downfall walk
Chapter 4 page 167

Three Shires Bridge, Three Shires Head
walk Chapter 5 page 170

Rudyard Lake walk
Chapter 5 page 171

Recommended Maps

Ordnance Survey maps covering this guide:
Touring Map and Guide N° 4 - Peak District. 1 inch to 1 mile scale
Sheet N° 119 - Buxton, Matlock and Dovedale - 1:50,000 scale
Outdoor Leisure Sheet N° 1 - The Peak District - Dark Peak Area. 1:25,000 scale
Outdoor Leisure Sheet N° 24 - The Peak District - White Peak Area. 1:25,000 scale

Harveys Superwalker maps.
With greater detail for hill walkers and orienteers:
Dark Peak North. 1:25,000 scale
Dark Peak South. 1:25,000 scale

Harveys Walker's Maps.
General purpose maps for walkers and 'off road' cyclists.
Dark Peak North. 1:40,000 scale
Dark Peak South. 1:40,000 scale

Bartholomew Walking Guides.
Many of the walks, all of which are suitable for families, and described in this book, are covered in greater detail together with maps, by the following guides:
Walk the Peak District; 40 walks selected and described by Brian Spencer.
Best walks in the Peak District, Fully mapped guide to 15 scenic walks.

Goldeneye cyclist's map.
Showerproof, tear resistant, easy to follow with lively, bright, illustrated covers and a comprehensive index:
Peak District Cycling Map. 2 miles to 1 inch, (1:126,720 scale)

Goldeneye Map-Guides.
Road maps suitable for motorists and cyclists.
Peak District. 2 miles to 1 inch. Combined tourist leisure map and guide.
Magical and Mystery Tours in and around the Peak District. 2 miles to 1 inch.
A selection of scenic drives. Clear text and overprinted routes.

Chapter 1

Solomon's Temple
4¹/₂ miles - Easy; Uphill Sections - 2 hours

Solomon's Temple has one of the finest views over this part of the Peak.
Leave the car at Buxton Country Park, near Poole's Cavern. Walk back along the road in the direction of Buxton. Turn right along a gap between houses and cross a series of fields, aiming towards a further group of houses. Turn right here and climb a stepped-stile then turn left to follow a wall, uphill. Keep to the right of the large house in front and also the group of trees to its rear. Go over the crest of the hill. Reaching the road, bear left for a few yards then right and go through a gate to follow a farm track. Go through the farmyard and out along its access track, across the open limestone moor. Climb up to the road and turn right for about ¹/₄ mile. Go left at a signpost, uphill along a cart track, past an untidy group of farm buildings. Follow the direction of a second signpost and aim for the prominent tower of Solomon's Temple. Bear left in front of the tower and go downhill to a wall. Squeeze through a narrow stile. Turn left when you reach the next boundary wall and walk into the woods. A woodland path descends to a flight of steps leading directly to the car park.

Miller's Dale
5 miles - Moderate - 3 hours

Upland pastures contrast with almost hidden limestone dales on this walk.
Park at Miller's Dale Station. Walk downhill along the road and turn left at the junction. Go under the twin viaducts and follow the road, past the Anglers' Rest, then turn left up a side lane for about 80yds. Turn left on to a stony track, following it to the rear of a farm. Go through a gate behind the farmhouse and along a steadily ascending walled track. Continue along this high level track until it reaches a narrow road and turn left. Go downhill by road, across Monk's Dale. When the road begins to climb, look out for a stone stile on the left. Go through it

and climb the grassy path until it joins a walled track. Turn left where the track forks and continue with it when it becomes a path crossing a series of narrow fields. Cross a stone stile and then walk diagonally left across the long narrow final field into Wormhill village. Bear left to follow the road through the village, downhill into a shallow depression. Turn right at the bottom of the dip, to follow a signpost, past a cottage, downhill through a rocky dell. Follow the narrow path down the steep, scrub covered hillside as far as the river. Do not cross, but turn left to follow the riverbank downstream. Turn left when you reach the road, uphill on a path waymarked to the station.

Tideswell, Miller's & Cressbrook Dales
7¹/₂ miles - Moderate; one 400ft climb - 3-3¹/₂ hours

Considered the finest of the eastern dales. The walk starts at the car park in Tideswell Dale. Follow the well defined path downstream. Turn left along the road to Litton Mill. Go through the mill yard and bear right, then left along the dale bottom path, beside a tranquil pond in Water-cum-Jolly Dale. Cross the start of an old mill race and go through the yard at Cressbrook Mill. Turn left at the road, forking right after a few yards. Climb with the road then go to the right along a wooded lane to Ravensdale Cottages. Keep to the left of the cottages and climb steadily through woodland and out into the rocky, treeless upper reaches of Cressbrook Dale. Walk beneath the towering outcrop of Peter's Stone and on towards a stone cottage, keeping to the left of its barn. Turn left at the busy main road, then after 100yds, go through a stone stile on the left. Follow the path uphill to the Litton road. Walk through the village and down to the Tideswell Dale road. Turn left at the junction to reach the car park.

Monsal Dale
6¹/₂ miles - Easy - 3¹/₂ hours

Gentle paths lead to the spectacular viewpoint of Monsal Head.
From the sports field in Ashford-in-the-

Water, follow a signposted path uphill to the top road. Leaving the upper houses and a farm behind, turn right to cross a field, then cross a second road to follow a walled path signposted to Little Longstone. Follow the path, crossing a side road after about a quarter of a mile, then over fields to reach the old railway track, now known as the Monsal Trail. Follow yellow 'M' waymarks, to the right and over fields into Little Longstone. Turn left at the road, past the Pack Horse Inn, and onwards to Monsal Head. Go through a stile to cross the left of the car park in front of the café. Take the second path and go down the scrub covered hillside and as far as the river. Cross the footbridge and turn left. Go downstream then carefully across the busy A6, through the car park and picnic site, then over a stile to follow a path marked 2,3,8. Cross a wooden stile and go through a gap in a low limestone crag. Bear left and onto the wooded hillside beyond Demon's Dell. Cross another stile and follow a well made woodland path slanting towards the river. Go past the outflow of a mine sough, and two partly restored small water mills, and along the valley bottom, through fields as far as a side road. Turn left then right at the main road to follow its grassy verge. Cross the road opposite the old bridge back into Ashford.

Ashford Lake
5¹/₂ miles - Easy - 3 hours

The 'lake' referred to in this walk, is a lovely stretch of water created by damming the Wye downstream of Ashford-in-the-Water to power Bakewell mills built by Richard Arkwright.
Starting in Bakewell, follow the main road north-west from the town centre, past the fire station, then turn right over a narrow packhorse bridge. Take the winding lane opposite, uphill, through a metal gate and into fields. Reaching the Monsal Trail, turn left along the old railway. Cross a bridge and walk on until a signpost indicates a path to your right. Go down the embankment and turn right towards the road. Go under the bridge and walk forwards to the junction with another road. Cross this road and walk up the farm lane

opposite. Go past the farm, then follow a signpost to the left, and right around Churchdale Hall. Cross a stile, go downhill to the road and turn left when you reach the A6020 road. On the outskirts of Ashford, follow a path on the right past cottages and into the main part of the village. Turn left along the side road back to and over the A6020 at the junction. Cross an abandoned road bridge and turn left with the A6 for about 80yds, then left through a kissing gate. Follow the path above the river, past Ashford Lake, uphill through a housing estate. Follow macadamed paths through the estate, then bear right up a narrow field and back to the A6. Turn left and follow the road as far as the entrance to the second factory on the left. Cross its access bridge and bear right along a side lane, past the turning to the packhorse bridge, and right at another kissing gate. Take the field path across the water meadows and into Bakewell.

Chelmorton & Deepdale
4¹/₄ miles - Moderate; rocky in Deepdale - 2¹/₂ hours

Contrasting with aptly named Deepdale, another feature of this walk is the preserved field system near Chelmorton which dates from medieval times.

The walk starts at the cross roads below Chelmorton's Church Inn. With your back to the pub, turn right and walk down the lane, past narrow fields. Cross the road and take the right hand of two tracks, following it to the lower fields. Go through a stile and over a meadow, past Burrs Farm, following a grassy path all the while. Taking care, go down the slippery, tree-shaded, rocky path into the dale bottom. Turn left in the valley and follow the perimeter of the old quarry. Bear left where the dale forks, to follow a wide, grassy path along the bottom of Horseshoe Dale. Climb uphill along an ancient monastic path, Priest's Way, and into a stockyard. Go through a bridlegate and turn left along the road. Follow it for about 400yds beyond the turning to Chelmorton. Turn right opposite a corrugated iron shed and walk along a narrow field access path. Follow this path through the ancient field system, back into Chelmorton.

Youlgreave & Lathkill Dale
8 miles - Easy/Moderate - 4¹/₂ hours

Lathkill Dale is a delight throughout the year.

Parking can usually be found in the centre of Youlgreave. The walk starts opposite the hall where a side lane drops quickly down to Bradford Dale. Follow this past a cottage selling teas, over a clapper bridge and turn right along the dale bottom. Turn right to cross a wide bridge, then bear left uphill to the road. Turn right at the road, following it as far as the second bend. Turn left and go through a narrow stile. Climb with the field path to reach the upper road by a step-stile. Ignoring the path opposite, turn left for about 50yds until a stile on the right gives access to a path leading to Moor Lane picnic site. Turn left along the road and ahead at the junction. Climb a wall stile on the right and cross a series of large fields, following occasional waymark posts. Bear right, then left with signposts around Calling Low Farm, then half right and begin to go downhill to the lip of Cales Dale. Go down the steep, often slippery path and into the dale bottom. Turn right to reach Lathkill Dale. Cross a footbridge and turn right, following the riverside path along wooded Lathkill Dale. Notice the old sign indicating a concessionary path and bear right when you reach Lathkill Lodge. Turn left beside the often dry river bed and go past the front of the house, along the dale as far as Conksbury Bridge. Turn right to cross the bridge, then follow the road for 120yds as far as a stile on the left. Go through this and walk through fields to the old lane beside Raper Lodge. Turn right and climb the lane, bearing left when it joins a minor road, back into Youlgreave.

Elton & Robin Hood's Stride
3 miles - Easy - 1¹/₂ - 2 hours

From a village where lead miners once lived, the walk visits Robin Hood's Stride, a gritstone crag which, at twilight looks like a large house, giving the outcrop its alternative name, 'Mock Beggar's Hall'. Street parking can usually be found near Elton church. Turn right and walk down the lane beside the church. Fork left at the Old

Rectory and follow a field path, downhill and across the valley. Cross a minor road and go through the stile opposite to follow a path leading past Tomlinson Wood. Follow a line of telegraph poles away from the wood, then left at a cart track. Turn right to cross a ditch marked by a footpath sign. Incline left up the field, over a stile and into mixed woodland. Follow a track through the wood until it reaches a road and turn right, uphill. Go left on to a signposted path and aim for the prominent rocks of Robin Hood's Stride. A side path on the left of the rocks leads to a hermit's cave at the foot of Cratcliff Rocks. Return to the depression between the two sets of rocks and go downhill towards the road. Do not follow the main road, but bear right on to a narrower side lane, following it uphill past a large house. Turn right at a signpost and then go half left, uphill on to a sparsely wooded slope. Bear right at the perimeter fence of a sports ground and follow it back to Elton's main street. The church is to the left.

Chapter 2

Carl Wark & Higger Tor
3³/₄ miles - Moderate - 2 hours

Carl Wark is one of the enigmas of the Peak. Rather than the usual earth banked fortification, this prehistoric camp has stone walls.
Park at the car park on Longshaw Estate. Follow a woodland path, over the B6521 and on to the A625. Turn left along this road, round the bend as far as the Toad's Mouth rock. Cross a fence stile on the Hathersage side of the rock to follow an upward path across the moor. Aim for the prominent knoll of Carl Wark. Go through the camp's fortifications then down to and across a broad col. Climb up to Higger Tor's rocky skyline. Scramble through the summit rocks and bear right, following a moorland path parallel to the Fiddler's Elbow road. Cross Upper Burbage Bridge then immediately turn right, through a gate to follow a green track, gently downhill past abandoned old gritstone quarries as far as the main road.

Turn left at the road then, either return along the outward path back to Longshaw, or divert via the Fox House Inn.

Stanage Edge
7 miles - Moderate - 3-4 hours

This walk is through countryside steeped in the legend of Robin Hood and Little John.
From Hathersage car park, take the path towards the main street. Cross the road and follow the lane opposite until it joins a path to the church. Turn right for the church where Little John is buried. Left out of the lych gate and follow a lane. Go through a gate and keep to the right through a field, following a garden boundary. Through a kissing gate then left along a farm lane as far as a cattle grid. Turn right, go through a gate and follow a line of trees towards Toothill Farm, bearing right along the farm track. Left at a metalled road as far as a bend, then follow a walled track, steadily climbing to the open moors. Cross a fence stile and climb the moorland path. Go left when you reach the road, as far as its junction with the Ladybower road. Left at the 'Open Country' sign and aim for the prominent Cowper Stone. Climb the outcrop to its left and follow a fairly level path along the top of Stanage Edge. Turn left at a break in the crags and walk downhill on a flagged path leading to a toilet block. Go to the left, then right, downhill on a woodland path to North Lees Hall and go down its access drive. Turn right at the road to follow it for a short way until a gate on the left points the way to a signposted field track. Follow this into Hathersage.

Eyam & Black Harry
5 miles - Easy - 2¹/₂ hours

Black Harry was an 18th century highwayman who lived on the moors above Eyam, the plague village.
From the old market square in Eyam, follow Lydgate out of the village, then left on to a path signposted to Stoney Middleton. Go downhill to the latter, then cross the road and climb the tarmac path beside the Royal

Oak. Turn right along a minor road for a few yards, then left on to a side lane towards a large house. Go to the right of the house, and follow a boundary wall. Cross a stile and bear left across a series of meadows, then down a scrubby hillside, (slippery when wet) into Coombs Dale. Turn right along the track, following it past Sallet Hole Mine where fluorspa was mined. About half a mile beyond the mine a stile on the right leads to a path climbing to a track from Black Harry Gate. (Do not worry if you miss the stile, a right turn at the next track junction will join Black Harry Gate track at its start). Cross the quarry road, diagonally right and go down a rough track. Bear right, then left downhill past Darlton Quarry to the main road. Cross the A623 with care and climb the tree shaded road opposite back into Eyam.

Curbar & Froggatt Edges
10 miles - Moderate - 5-6 hours

Paths around Big Moor link with gritstone edges high above the Derwent Valley.
Park at Curbar Gap (map ref: 261 748). Follow the path south along the top of Baslow Edge, past the Eagle Stone, until it joins a track climbing from Baslow. Turn left and follow it to the road. Turn right here, then left at its junction with the A621. Walk along the grassy verge until a reservoir track leads off to the left. Follow this, climbing steadily up to Barbrook reservoir, then right along the track from it, until a finger post on the left indicates a moorland path. Take this until, within sight of the B6054, a concessionary path parallel to the road, links with a path crossing the moor from the west. Turn left along it, down to the road and the Grouse Inn. Follow the road to the left, away from the front of the inn for about three quarters of a mile, then go through a gate on the left and climb up to Froggatt Edge. Follow the escarpment back to Curbar Gap and the car park.

Birchen Edge
4 miles - Moderate - 2 hours

Two monoliths, erected in memory of Nelson and Wellington, make excellent markers for this walk.

Park beside the Robin Hood Inn off the A619 Chesterfield road and walk past the adjoining cottage. Climb a ladder stile on the left and follow a rocky, woodland path for a couple of hundred yards or so, then choose one of the climbers' paths leading up to Birchen Edge. Turn left along the top of the escarpment, past Nelson's Monument with its view over Chatsworth, and as far as a triangulation pillar. Go half left here then right along a moorland path heading towards the busy A621 Sheffield road. Climb a ladder stile and turn left and down to the main road. Cross this and follow a minor road opposite as far as a gate leading on to a turf covered moorland track. Follow the track, past Wellington's Monument until it reaches a moorland boundary wall. Do not go through the gate, but turn sharp left, downhill into oak woodland. Cross Bar Brook by a narrow footbridge and climb up to the A621. Cross over and look for a horse trough beside Cupola Cottage. A path directly above it leads through scattered birch wood, then over a stretch of moor to a stile giving access to the A619. The Robin Hood Inn is to the left.

Chatsworth
6 miles - Easy - 3 hours

Walkers are free to enjoy Chatsworth's parkland and woods and this walk takes advantage of that opportunity.
Park at Calton Lees south of Chatsworth and follow the road towards Beeley. Cross the narrow road bridge and immediately go through a kissing gate on the right. Walk across the meadow and into Beeley village. Go to the right of the church and turn right then left through the village. Walk beside Beeley Brook, but where the surfaced lane bears right, go forwards up a grassy path. Go through a gate on the right and into the forest, then follow a track steadily uphill. Still in the forest, bear left and cross the stream above a small waterfall. Cross a stone stile and bear left along a sandy lane as far as the bend. Climb the stepped stile next to a gate and follow the moorland track on the left up to the forest boundary. Climb another step stile and walk through the forest, bearing left at the next junction. Follow the

track with its views of Chatsworth House and its gardens below . Pass Emperor Lake and then left at another junction to reach the Hunting Tower. Go down steps below the tower, over a forest road, then left at the next to reach the Children's Farm. Keep to the left here, along the north front of Chatsworth, (refreshments here) and down to the bridge. Cross over and follow the river downstream as far as the ruined mill. Bear right here and back to the car park.

Stanton Moor
4¼ miles - Easy - 2 hours

Numerous ancient cairns and henges indicate that Stanton Moor was once far more important than now.

This easy walk starts and finishes at Birchover's renowned Druid Inn. Cross the road at the bend opposite the inn and follow a woodland path uphill. Turn left opposite the quarry entrance to follow the road for about 300 yards. Turn right beneath a beech tree and go past a large boulder to follow a sandy path on to the moor. Turn left at the aptly named Cork Stone, then right to follow a moorland path past the triangulation column. Continue to Nine Ladies Stone Circle and turn right along the moor edge, past the Earl Grey Memorial Tower. Follow the edge then bear left downhill to the road. Turn right for 200 yards then left at a stile beneath an oak. Keep to the left of the farm, then ahead along a field path. Go through a stile beside a gate and turn right on to a farm lane. Turn left and almost immediately right at Uppertown to follow a bridleway as far as Rocking Stone Farm, a large stone house. Go through a stile on the right prior to the house, down its access drive and along a lane to Birchover.

Winster
5½ miles - Easy - 2½ hours

Winster is a haphazard cluster of houses and narrow alleys, or jitties as they are known locally. The walk crosses fields where Winster miners once dug for lead ore.

Parking is difficult in the village, but there is usually space on the road to the Miner's Standard Inn.

Walk up the side street from the Market House and turn left at Hope Cottage. Follow a path signposted to Bonsall, diagonally left and uphill across the fields. Bear left above the village then right to reach the upper fields. Turn left at the top road as far as a weight restriction sign, then left down the first of two adjacent tracks. Keeping to the right of the farm, follow blue waymarks above a quarry. Bear right downhill and away from the quarry, heading for a ruined barn. Turn left along a walled track. Cross the dry dale and climb to the right towards the village. Follow a side lane left to the main street. Cross the road and keeping to the right of the cottage opposite, follow the path signposted to Stanton Moor and Birchover. Cross two fields and turn left along a woodland track. Climb over a stile and turn left along a forest track. Do not immediately go down to the nearby stream, but follow it along the valley for about half a mile. Cross the stream and go over a stile, then climb uphill using old gateposts and stone stiles to keep to the pathless route. Climb the last stile and turn right along the road into Winster.

High Tor & the Heights of Abraham
4½ miles - Easy - 2-2½ hours

Here is an almost alpine walk climbing two steep limestone hillsides. The longest of the two climbs can be avoided by using the cable car to the Heights of Abraham where there is a restaurant and other amenities.

Walk along the riverside path through Matlock's Hall Leys Park and as far as the railway bridge. Turn left at the bridge and go up a cobbled lane to the entrance to High Tor grounds. Follow the path over the summit then bear right on the other side, down to the lower station of the Heights of Abraham cable car. Take this across the valley and from its upper station, bear right away from the restaurant and cavern. Go through a stile and turn left, uphill. Left again on to a level path through beech woodland as far as Ember Farm. Follow its access track downhill into Bonsall. Bear right into the centre of the village and its stepped cross. Turn right opposite the cross and the King's Head Inn, to climb a track. Bear left at the top along a walled path, then right at the junction with another. Uphill along a grassy track towards open fields as far as a stile on the right. Go through this and over a couple of fields. Cross a gravel lane to go through another stile. Bear right and begin to go downhill, across a rough track and down a field to the left of Masson Farm. Continue downhill, heading for Matlock below.

Cromford & Black Rocks
4¹/₂ miles - Easy/Moderate; one 530ft climb - 2¹/₂ hours

This is a walk for historical railway buffs and anyone interested in industrial archaeology. Follow the canal towpath from Cromford as far as High Peak Junction. Cross and climb the steep incline as far as the car park at Black Rocks. Turn right here and go through a clearing to the bottom of a wooded slope. Climb up to the boundary wall and over a stile. Follow the path next to a boundary wall, keeping to the left of the house in front. Go through a narrow gate and turn left, downhill along the drive. Go through a squeezer stile on the right to follow a walled path into the upper limits of Cromford. Turn left at the road and follow it downhill into the village. Cross the main A6 and go down Mill Lane, past Arkwright's Mill as far as the turning into the canal car park.

Chapter 3

Brand Top
3 miles - Moderate - 1¹/₂ hours

This walk is around a little known area of upper Dovedale. Many of the paths were once used by packhorse traders. Access to Brand Top (map ref: 045 685), is along a signposted minor road from the A53 over Axe Edge.

Park carefully near the war memorial in Brand Top and walk down the road towards the valley. Turn right on what has become a track and then left, almost down to the stream. Follow a path downstream along a grassy terrace, then steeply into a side valley. Climb a stile and cross the stone foot bridge and, still walking downstream, follow a cobbled bridleway. Do not cross the packhorse bridge at Tenterhill, but turn left and cross a stile. Go past a barn and bear left uphill over three rough fields. Follow a wall as far as Leycote Farm, then away along its access track. Keep to the right of Booth Farm, as far as its duckpond. Turn left here, cross a stile, and walk back towards the farm. Follow a fence away and use stiles to cross field boundaries. Go over a rise then continue ahead and slightly uphill at a fingerpost along an improving track. Turn left away from the track. There is no path, but follow a wall and cross a plank bridge. Bear right up the shallow valley. Turn left over a footbridge. Ignoring the stile in front, turn sharp right and follow a wire fence uphill. Go to the right along a farm lane, then right again for Brand Top.

Biggin & Iron Tors
6¹/₂ miles - Easy - 3 hours

The walk is from Biggin, high above Dovedale which is reached along Biggin Dale and followed as far as Iron Tors. The return is by way of the Tissington Trail.
Take the side road south past Biggin church and bear right at its end. Go through a stile on the left to cross two fields, aiming for a gap in a group of cottages. Left along the road for 100 yds, then right at a stile and head downhill into Biggin Dale. Turn left and follow the dale until it joins the Dove. Turn left along the riverbank. A few yards beyond a footbridge, turn left and climb the craggy side dale. Bear right at the dale head, along a road as far as the railway bridge. Turn right and climb the embankment, then left along the trail. Leave the trail where it crosses an unsurfaced track, by turning left, down to, then over the track. Following yellow waymarks, stile and gates, walk towards Biggin which is reached along a walled lane. The church and pub are to the right.

Hartington & its Dales
5 miles - Easy/Moderate - 3 hours

Hartington has always been a busy village and is mentioned in *Domesday* as 'Hortedun'. Izaak Walton stayed nearby at the home of Charles Cotton.
From the village square walk as far as the

war memorial and turn right up the steep side road. Turn right above the youth hostel, along a walled track to its end. Go over a stile and turn half right to cross two fields, aiming for a clump of trees. Climb the stile and turn left along the lane as far as a crossroads. Walk on along a rough cart track. Beyond a well-made stone barn, go through a gate and walk downhill into Biggin Dale. Turn right and follow the dale downhill into Dovedale. Turn right and follow a riverside path, upstream all the way to Beresford Dale. Cross the river by a footbridge and turn right to continue upstream, recrossing at Pike Pool. Climb away from the river and into fields and so into Hartington.

Viator's Bridge
2¼ miles - Easy - 1½ hours

The attractive packhorse bridge stands downstream of delightful little Milldale. Parking can be found above the village.
Walk downstream and cross the bridge, continuing along the riverbank. Turn left within sight of the Dove Holes caves, up the wooded side dale as indicated by a signpost to Alsop-en-le-Dale. Turn left at the dale head and in the direction of Hanson Grange Farm. Join its access lane about 100 yds above the farm. At the end of a partly walled section of lane, turn left as indicated by a signpost towards Milldale. Zigzags of an old packhorse way make the going easier on the last stages.

Dovedale
6½ miles - Moderate; one 538 ft climb - 3-4 hours

This walk visits some of the best known features of Dovedale.
From Dovedale car park follow the signposted path towards Ilam across fields behind the Izaak Walton Hotel. Do not join the road, but turn sharp right to follow the path beneath Bunster Hill passing the remains of St Bertram's Well. At the top of the slope cross two adjoining stiles. Aim for the prominent tree ahead. Go to the right, then left through two field gates beside a stone barn. Follow the track on the right of the barn until it joins another. Turn right

and walk towards Air Cottage, keeping to its right, then left along the valley crest. Join a farm track beyond the cottage until it passes a stile on the right. Climb over it into woodland then bear left and begin to go downhill. Follow the path steeply downhill to the river. Turn right in the valley bottom and cross over by the footbridge beneath Ilam Rock. Turn right and follow the river back to Dovedale stepping stones and the car park.

Longnor Two Valleys walk
4 miles - Easy - 2 hours

The old market centre of Longnor sits on a broad ridge between the Dove and Manifold valleys. This walk visits both by using little known paths.
From Longnor's old market place, follow the road east for about 150 yds. Turn right along the signposted lane to Folds End Farm. Go left through the farmyard. Climb a stone stile and turn half right to follow a path down to the River Manifold. Turn left along a farm track and keep left through the farmyard, then right along a rutted track. Follow it past one gate, then through the second. Take a track uphill to the road and turn right for about 500 yds. Climb a stone stile on the left and cross three fields. Turn right to follow the track towards Under Whitle Farm. Go over a stile on the left above the farm garden and follow yellow waymark arrows and stiles to keep to the faint path across a series of fields. Continue down to the River Dove and follow it upstream, still using the waymarks. Cross the river by a footbridge and follow a track as far as the lane into Crowdecote. Turn right at the road, then left along a side lane. Turn left at a signpost, along a lane into open fields. Turn left at the next junction and go back to the river. Cross Beggar's Bridge and begin to climb the valley side. Bear left at a barn and follow the gravel lane from it into Longnor.

Thor's Cave
4 miles - Moderate; one climb of 295 ft 2-3 hours

High above the Manifold Thor's Cave was the home of our prehistoric ancestors.

Park in Wetton village and follow the main street past the church until it turns left. Follow the signpost pointing to 'Back of Wetton'. Cross a series of fields below Wetton Hill, then over a stream and head for a belt of trees. Right along a track then left at the junction with a second. When this track turns right, go left to follow a boundary wall downhill. Move to the right then back by an awkward stile to avoid dense scrub. Go down the dry valley and through the stockyard of Dale Farm into the Manifold Valley. Turn left along the valley road, then right and left to cross the river, then follow the old railway. Look out for Thor's Cave on the hillside to your left and go over a footbridge to begin the signposted climb to the cave (NB. slippery when wet). From the cave follow the concessionary path back to Wetton.

Ilam Hall
4¹/₂ miles - Easy - 2¹/₂ hours

A quiet riverside stroll is contrasted with a woodland and upland pasture ramble.
From Ilam Hall follow the river, upstream past one bridge, then left to cross the second. Ignoring a path forking right, bear left uphill on a pathless course towards the trees. Use a stile to keep to the route. Turn left on a grassy track, following a boundary wall. Cross a dry valley and aim for the broad track curving uphill around wooded Hazleton Clump. Climb an awkward stile and turn left along the road. Follow it over Blore cross roads to Coldwall Farm. Turn left from the road and follow a path on the left of the farm, downhill along a wide grassy track. Do not cross Coldwall Bridge, but turn left and follow the riverside path back to Ilam.

Carsington Pasture
6³/₄ miles - Easy/Moderate; one 333 ft climb - 3¹/₂ hours

Ancient miners' tracks lead to an airy viewpoint over Carsington Water
From the west end of Carsington village where the road turns sharply left, turn right along a short lane. Climb steps on the right of the last house and zigzag up the steep hillside, aiming for the top right hand corner. Do not go over the stile, but turn left and follow the boundary wall. Cross the road by a couple of stiles and turn left along the High Peak Trail. At Longcliffe Wharf turn right, then left along the road. Walk down the road until it bends right, then go through a gate on the left. Keep to the left of a barn and using stiles, cross the limestone moor. Cross the head of an access lane and walk across a rocky field to reach Brassington. Turn left at the main street and pass the Gate Inn, then the Miners' Standard at the next junction. Cross the road and bear right through the farmyard opposite. Go through a stile and turn right to cross three narrow fields, bearing left and uphill at the last one. Right at the next stile and walk round the grassy hillside. Cross the lane and climb a couple of fields, aiming to the left of a group of tree shrouded rocks and go over the brow of the hill. Follow an improving track down to Carsington.

Roystone Grange
4¹/₂ miles - Easy - 2 hours

This walk visits a farming settlement whose occupation can be traced from prehistoric times to the present day.
From Minning Low car park, follow the High Peak Trail to the left through woodland. Climb left at a fingerpost then over a stile to cross a series of fields. Over a stile and left along a lane, following waymarks. Cross the road and go down the lane opposite. Right at the next junction to follow the lane to Roystone Grange Farm and through its farmyard. After visiting the medieval and Roman remains below the modern farm, walk back towards the farm and prior to the farmyard, turn right to cross a stile. Follow the path across a grassy depression. Cross a stone stile on the left then turn right uphill and under an old railway bridge. Go forwards as far as a lane and turn left along it to reach the High Peak Trail. Turn right along the trail to reach the car park.

Chapter 4

Grindsbrook Skyline
5¹/₂ miles - Strenuous; one 1210 ft climb
4-5 hours

Here is a walk to sample the rigours of Kinder Scout. Although it should be easy to follow, the walk must not be attempted in bad weather or mist.

From the car park below Edale station, walk along the road past the National Park Information Centre and into the village. Continue along the lane and cross Grindsbrook. Bear left to follow the wide path past a stone barn, then fork right and uphill towards Herdman's Plantation. Climb the stile on the left of the trees and walk uphill on a well made path. Keep left at the next junction and climb beneath the rocks of Ringing Roger to reach the head of Golden Clough. Turn left at a large cairn and follow the escarpment path over numerous streams. On reaching another large cairn, go forwards a little way then bear left along the skyline path. Aim for the prominent hump of Grindslow Knoll. Go steeply downhill to a stile in the moorland boundary wall. Climb this and follow a field path, gradually leftwards into Edale.

Rushup Edge
5¹/₂ miles - Moderate/Strenuous;
one 1029 ft climb - 3¹/₂ hours

The climb to the summit of Rushup Edge is amply rewarded by the superb views.

From Edale Station, walk towards the village until the road bends right. Turn left and cross a stile to follow a waymarked route across three fields. Cross the railway bridge and then right at the road, following it through Barber Booth. Cross the river and turn right along the valley bottom road. Climb a stile on the left and follow a field path towards Manor House Farm, but keep well to its right by using stiles in boundaries. Turn right at the intake wall, along the sunken track known locally as Chapel Gate, steeply uphill. Bear half left at a signposted path junction and continue across the moor. Left at the next signpost to follow the broad ridge of Rushup Edge.

Go down to the road at Mam Nick and turn left, downhill until a wicket gate on the right gives access to a path downhill on the left. Go down this and to the right of a farmhouse, then out along its access drive to the Edale road.

Castleton & Mam Tor
6 miles - Moderate/Strenuous;
total ascent: 1095 ft   3-4 hours

This is a walk with ever changing views and interesting features. If Castleton is crowded, the walk can easily be joined at the car park below Mam Nick.

From the car park in Castleton turn right at the Bull's Head and go past the National Park Information Centre. Bear left at the top of the street, then right through a narrow gap between cottages and into Cave Dale. Follow the path to the head of the dale, then left with it across the moor to a track junction. Turn right and right again along a track running beside Rowter Farm. Cross the road and go over Windy Knoll to reach a second road. Bear left then right here to climb the steep, rough pasture up to Mam Nick. Cross one of the stiles next to the road and climb to the top of Mam Tor. Walk downhill along a wide path and then turn right at Hollins Cross. Follow the path steeply downhill until, it joins a farm road. Turn left and follow it into Castleton.

Win Hill
5 miles - Easy/Moderate;
one 966ft climb - 3 hours

Win Hill's shapely summit rises above Ladybower Reservoir. The ascent from Yorkshire Bridge is steep, but once gained, everything is downhill from there!

Park off the main road in Yorkshire Bridge and walk down the side road into the valley bottom. Turn right at the bridge, then left at a signpost and climb steeply up Parkin Clough. Above the clough and beyond the last trees, the angle eases and the way is clear to the top of Win Hill. Follow the broad moorland ridge away from the summit until the path reaches the forest boundary. Follow the wall until a doorlike gate on the right marks the way into the forest. Walk downhill to the reservoir and turn right to follow the service track as far as the dam. Walk down the access road from the dam to the road junction and turn left for Yorkshire Bridge.

Ladybower
6¹/₂ miles - Moderate; one 580ft climb
3¹/₂ hours

This is a walk of contrasting views ranging from a man-made lake to distant moorland. Park at Fairholmes car park. Walk down the lane below the dam and continue with it along the eastern shore of Ladybower until it reaches the main road. Turn right and cross the viaduct then turn right for a short way along the reservoir road. Go through a narrow gate on the left and climb diagonally, to the right, across three fields. Go through two small gates next to a barn at Crookhill Farm, then ahead and left through a larger gate following a cart track. Climb a ladder stile and cross a couple of fields. Leave by a bridle gate and on to the open moor. Follow a grassy track waymarked by posts and aim for the upper edge of the forest. Keep to the left of the boundary. Turn right at a track junction and go past Lockerbrook Farm for about 200 yds, then right to go down a concessionary path into the forest. Follow yellow markers back to Fairholmes.

Kinder Downfall
8 miles - Strenuous; one 1247 ft climb, boggy sections 5-6 hours

This is the classic route on to Kinder and one that must only be attempted in clear weather. It starts from Bowden Bridge car park, where the mass trespass to Kinder began on 24 April 1932.
Follow the reservoir road away from the car park and turn right at the access gates then over the bridge. Follow the lane uphill past the farm. Go left, downhill and across the valley, then right and uphill along a rocky path above the filter houses. Right on to a path contouring above the reservoir, then down to the stream at its head. Bear left upstream to a broad moorland saddle and turn right. Climb to the edge of Kinder and turn right to follow the escarpment as far as the Downfall. Cross the rocky stream

bed and begin to go downhill along a moorland path. Turn sharp right at the next major stream, then right again across a depression, following a clear path downhill. Ahead at a path crossing and follow a wall down to a stile. Cross and descend through improving farmland, using stiles and gates as necessary. Keep to the left then right to pass Tunstead Clough Farmhouse. Follow the access drive into the valley bottom and turn right; following the lane back to the car park.

Langsett
3³/₄ miles - Easy - 2 hours

Here is an ideal moorland walk for a hot summer's day. From shaded woodland, the path climbs easily on to breezy moorland. It starts from the restored barn and National Park Information Centre by the side of the A616 in Langsett.
Follow the woodland path to the right from the car park, towards the head of the reservoir. Left at the track junction , then over a stone bridge and climb towards the open moor. Look out for the next (unsignposted) turning to the left at a wide gap in the ruined wall. Go past a farm ruin above the south side of the reservoir, then through a metal gate to follow a track between two sections of pine forest. Ahead where the track's surface is concrete, and ahead again as it joins the road. Go through Upper Midhope then left at the road junction, down to and over the dam wall, past the Waggon and Horses and into Langsett.

Binn Green
8¹/₂ miles - Strenuous, (some scrambling involved) - 6 hours

This exciting walk traverses a high moorland edge above the Saddleworth reservoirs. Care should be taken when scrambling above the waterfalls of Birchin Clough which can become dangerous under icy conditions. Park at Binn Green picnic area and walk down through trees to the reservoir access road. Turn left and follow it above Dovestone Reservoir to its end by the dam of Yeoman Hey Reservoir. Continue by track as far as the entrance to an underground aqueduct. A faint path to the half left enters steep Birchin Clough which is crossed and recrossed by boulders until a series of small but dramatic waterfalls will force you out on to the hillside to your left. Above the falls cross the stream and carefully climb the steep pathless hillside opposite to reach the moor edge. Turn right here to follow a steadily improving path, first past the Trinnacle, an outstanding outcrop of Raven Stones, then Ashway Cross. Above Great Dovestone Rocks a cairn and plaque are in memory of two local climbers killed in the Dolomites in 1972. The path continues along the edge, beyond the sturdy ruins of Bramley's Cot, an abandoned shooting cabin, to reach Chew Reservoir. Turn right here and go down the steep access road into the valley. Turn right above Dovestone Reservoir and follow a level path back to Yeoman Hey Reservoir. Cross the dam and turn left along the roadway back to Binn Green.

Lantern Pike
4¼ miles - Easy - 2/3 hours

Lantern Pike is an ideal vantage point covering the surrounding moors. The walk starts in Rowarth where the Little Mill Inn offers refreshment at the end of the day.
Go past the Little Mill Inn for about 200 yds and turn right at a signpost. Cross three fields to reach Thornsett Fields Farm. Do not use the farm lane, but continue ahead over a stile and follow a grassy path towards, then below a belt of trees to join a lane. Turn left uphill along the lane past Aspenshaw Hall, then ahead on the track above Feeding Hey Farm. Right at the next junction and downhill along a track until it joins a side road. Turn left for a quarter mile. Left at the end of a row of cottages to climb a farm track, then ahead at the junction. Continue by footpath from the lane end, over Lantern Pike and down to the junction of six tracks. Follow the post directing to Rowarth, down to Long Lee Farm. Left through the farmyard, then right downhill along a lane back to Rowarth.

Middle Moor & Little Hayfield
5 miles - Moderate - 2½ -3 hours

A valley stroll combined with a moorland ramble. Leave the car at Hayfield's main car park.
Go under the by-pass into Hayfield. Cross the bridge and follow the road left through the village, back under the by-pass. Walk past modern houses and turn right by a telephone box, along a tree shaded lane. Go past a group of cottages and over a narrow bridge. Climb through sparse woodland, keeping ahead at the next signpost. Bear left uphill along a gravel path behind an old farmhouse. Cross a stile on the right and follow a level path into woodland. Turn right at a signpost and into the side valley, past Brookhouse Farm and up to the main road and turn left. There is no footpath so keep to the right, facing traffic. Opposite a group of cottages, turn right and go through a gate, then right again to cross a footbridge. Climb the winding moorland path, past the white shooting cabin to a path junction. Turn right and follow the path downhill to Hayfield. Turn right at the road and follow it, bearing left for the bridge, then right to the car park.

Chapter 5

Shining Tor & Errwood Hall
6½ miles - Moderate;
(total ascent 896ft) 3½ hours

The scenery has changed from that of a hundred years ago when the Grimshaws lived at Errwood Hall. Now in ruins, it makes a sad reminder of times past.
Park beyond Shooter's Clough Bridge and follow the nature trail path away from the car park, uphill then over a stream to reach the ruined hall. Go past the hall and down to another stream, cross the footbridge and bear left, uphill. Follow the narrow path past the 'Shrine' and up to the road. Turn left along the road. Leave the road at the top of the rise and turn left, following a high level moorland path across the long ridge to Shining Tor. Turn left here and cross the valley, then left on reaching an old but

well made track. Bear right at the junction on to a path leading back to the car park.

Fernilee
5 miles - Moderate; one climb of 394ft
2-3 hours

Fernilee Reservoir is older than its neighbour, Errwood. Forest above the west bank is a good blend of pines and deciduous trees.

Park near Errwood dam and walk downstream to the west bank of Fernilee Reservoir, and follow it to its dam. Turn right along the road across the dam, then up to the main road and turn left for a little over 100yds. Go to the right along a farm lane for 80 yds then left over a stile. Walk towards the farm at the top of the field. From here go over a stile and turn right, along a lane for a few yards, then left on a field track as indicated by yellow waymarks. Right beyond the top of the first field and aim for the right-hand edge of the skyline wood. Over a stile and right along a lane for a quarter mile and right again over a stile where the lane bears left. Bear left downhill, over stiles as far as the main road. Turn right and go down the road for about 300 yds, as far as the bend. Left over a stile and bear left towards the top of a small wood, then right on a grassy path parallel to the main road. Climb a stile beside a clump of trees and follow a ruined wall, then over an open field to a ruin by a third clump. Left from the ruin, uphill to a signpost. turn right, downhill into a wooded valley. Cross the stream and up to the road, then turn right and follow it to the car park.

Chinley Churn
4¼ miles - Moderate; one steady climb of 774 ft - 2½ hours

Walled lanes lead to open moorland with views of the Cheshire Plain as well as the dramatic outline of Kinder Scout.

From a layby on the A6015 at Birch Vale, follow the moor road past a quarry entrance and as far as Moor Lodge. Continue along the unsurfaced track towards a track junction and turn left. Walk across the moor to a 'T' junction, then follow a wall across the moor, bearing left at a fingerpost and on to a grassy bridleway. Follow this downhill, through a gate and along the roughly surfaced lane. Left at the Grouse Inn and back to the layby.

South Head
4½ miles - Moderate - 2½ hours

The walk climbs the shapely dome of South Head from behind the Crown and Mitre in New Smithy at the junction of the Chinley and Hayfield roads.

Follow the lane behind the pub, then left at a 'No Through Road' sign, continuing uphill along a farm lane. Left at the farm and down to a stream. Turn right and climb a muddy path to the next farm, following its access lane until it turns left. Ahead on a grassy track, then right at a third farm to follow a cart track away. At a complex of track junctions go through the third gate to your right and along a rough cart track until it turns left over a stream. Continue ahead and cross a stile next to a narrow gate, then climb the steep grassy path. At the top of the slope, cross a stile and go right to cross a broad grassy saddle and the shoulder of South Head. Ahead at a footpath sign, then downhill along a track until it widens. Join a field track to the right, downhill into the valley. Reaching Shireoaks Farm, bear right and out along its access track, to a cluster of cottages and follow paths and byways to New Smithy.

Combs
4 miles - Easy - 2 hours

Combs is a village that hides itself away from the bustle of everyday life.

From the Beehive Inn in the centre of Combs, follow the Dove Holes road until it bears left. Turn right here along a farm lane as far as a bungalow near the entrance to Allstone Lee Farm. Follow a path signposted to White Hall, up the hillside, past Combshead Farm and to White Hall. Turn right along the lane past the hall as far as a house called Wainstones. Right here along a field track and down to Haylee Farm. Take the farm drive down to the road and turn right to follow it back to Combs.

Lyme Park, Bow Stones and Sponds Hill
5 miles - Easy- 2½ hours

This is a popular walk with unrivalled views of the western Peak District and the Cheshire Plain. Park below Lyme Hall and with the hall on your left follow a track into Knightslow Wood. Cross the park boundary wall and climb the moorland path to Bow Stones Farm. Turn right and follow a level track as far as a second gate and stile. Turn right to cross Sponds Hill, then go downhill towards the access drive of a solitary house. Do not go to the house, but cross a stile beside an old tree on the left and over a rough field, aided by waymarks. Join a farm lane on the left and follow it to a roadside chapel, then right and right again, down a drive to a lodge and gates on the right into West Park Woods. Follow the woodland track through the woods, then out into the park by way of a second gate and a track leading back to the hall.

Tegg's Nose
5 miles - Moderate; 492 foot descent and ascent - 3 hours

Tegg's Nose is a country park based on an old quarry. It makes an excellent viewpoint over the nearby 'Cheshire Alps'. A programme of guided walks runs throughout the year.
Follow the well-made path towards the quarry from the car park, and around the quarry rim. Turn left away from the main path, downhill into the valley bottom. Cross the dams of Teggsnose and Bottoms reservoirs and turn left at the road as far as Leather's Smithy Inn. Take the left-hand road for a quarter mile as far as a small car park and turn left along a forest track. Go left at a four-way signpost, and downhill. Follow a sign to Walker Barn to the right and uphill. Climb a stile on the forest boundary and over the road, then across a stile giving access to a path beside a large house. Cross two shallow valleys and go half-right. Keep to the left of Warrilowhead Farm and follow its drive to a right-hand bend. Bear left, downhill and across open fields. Go over an awkward stile and turn right along the lane to Walker Barn farmhouse, then left on a path leading to the Setter Dog Inn. Turn left away from the main road and follow the side road back to Tegg's Nose.

Macclesfield Forest & Shutlingsloe
7 miles - Strenuous; one 759 ft climb - 5 hours

Shutlingsloe is Cheshire's Matterhorn, arguably the most graceful peak in the Peak District.
From the layby above Trentabank Reservoir, follow the forest path signposted to Shutlingsloe. At the summit follow yellow waymarks downhill to the Crag Inn. Climb a flight of steps in the corner of the pub car park, then follow a grassy path as indicated by waymarks and stiles. Join a farm lane and follow it to the road. Turn right and walk to the bridge then right, cross a stile and follow waymarks above the stream as far as Oakenclough Farm. Turn left on the drive over the stream, then right along a moorland path to the Hanging Gate inn. Right at the pub and follow the minor road back to the reservoir.

Three Shires Head
4 miles - Easy - 2 hours

The walk starts in Flash, once the haunt of counterfeiters, then follows tracks once used by packhorse trains to reach a bridge where three counties meet.
Follow the road from Flash past the New Inn downhill to a sharp right-hand bend. Turn right along a concrete farm drive, but do not go into the farmyard. Left across a wooden footbridge and follow the sign to Three Shires Head. Left along the lane and down to the bridge. Go through the gate to the right of Three Shires Bridge and climb a stony track. Right over a single arched bridge and follow a track to the road. Right over a stone clapper bridge. Follow waymarks uphill across the heather moor and up to a wall, changing sides as indicated by stiles, then diagonally across the top of the hill. Right at a moorland track, then down a walled track into Flash.

Danebridge
4¹/₄ miles - Easy - 2¹/₂ hours

No Danes lived here, the word comes from the Old Welsh '*dan*', for a trickling stream.
The walk starts at Danebridge. Park carefully and walk south, up the road for about 50 yds, as far as a chapel, then left following a sign to Roach End. Follow waymarks through woodland and fields to Hanging Stone Farm. Keep to the left of the farm, then out along its access, past a second farm and left over a stile to climb to a gap in the moorland ridge. Bear right and follow a sign to Gradbach. Go down to the stream, but do not cross. Turn left and follow a woodland path signposted Danebridge, down the valley and, keeping to the left of Back Dane Farm, reach the road.

The Roaches
7 miles - Strenuous; one 608 ft climb - 4¹/₂ hours

These rocks are the highest in the Peak and are worth climbing if only to admire the view over North Staffordshire and the Cheshire Plain. There is a park and ride bus from Upper Hulme on summer weekends and Bank Holidays.
Start by climbing past Rockhall cottage, to the left and through the rocks towards the crest of the Roaches. Follow the escarpment as far as Roach End. Turn right and go past a cottage, bearing left into the forest. Follow the path round the hillside to Lud's Church, then on until you reach a gate. Do not go through, but turn left and follow the moorland path back to Roach End. Follow the lane back to the layby beneath Rockhall cottage.

Rudyard Lake
4¹/₂ miles - Easy - 2 hours

Rudyard Lake is in fact a reservoir built to supply water for the Caldon Canal between the Potteries and the Churnet Valley.
Park on the Leek side of Rudyard village. Walk towards the canal feeder and turn right. Follow it to the dam and climb left.

Follow the signposted track up to then along the western shore of the lake. At its head walk through the car park to reach the old railway. Turn right and follow the track back to the dam, then either walk into the village in search of refreshment, or retrace your steps back along the feeder.

Combes Valley
4 miles - Moderate - 3 hours

Combes Valley is a nature reserve with an interesting mix of wildlife from badgers to birds and woodland. Parking is available near the Warden's House on the road linking Cheddleton to the Leek-Ashbourne road.
Walk down the road from the car park and in the direction of Cheddleton. Left at the right-hand bend and follow a path down into and across the wooded valley. Go past Sharpcliffe Hall and out along its drive. Look for a path on the left and within sight of the lodge, turn left and follow a wall across rough pasture. Go to the right with it at its end, then left at a path junction, following the most direct path to Roughstone Hole Farm. Go to the left of the farm, down through woodland and over a footbridge. Climb to a group of buildings at Apesford and turn left along the road leading to the car park.

Scenic Car Drives

Prehistoric Peak

Around 20 miles
In this short drive you will find examples of the Peak District's history, ranging from its pre-history, through medieval to the present day.

The drive starts in Bakewell (church, Old House Museum, Market House, interesting buildings, restaurants, pubs, Monday market). Take the Monyash road as far as Bole Hill and turn right on the Chelmorton road, then left at the next junction, past Magpie Mine. Left again along a by-road into Monyash (church, cross on village green, miners' cottages, pub). Follow the Parsley Hay road to the junction almost at the A515 and turn sharp left past Arbor Low stone circle on the right. Pass Long Rake where fluorspa is worked on the site of an old lead mine. Turn right and follow the road into Middleton (attractive village; site of Bateman's Tomb, an early archaeologist). Left through the village and drive through Youlgreave (church, interesting buildings, pubs and restaurants). Through Alport and turn right on to the B5056, then left at the next side road, into Stanton in Peak (attractive village, pub), then across Stanton Moor (stone circles, cairns and tumuli), to Birchover (interesting houses, pubs). Back down the B5056 and follow it to the A6. Turn left past medieval Haddon Hall into Bakewell.

Western Dales & Moors

Around 41 miles
Using quiet by-roads, this route explores parts of upper Dovedale and the Manifold Valley.

The drive starts and finishes at Hartington's old railway station on the Tissington Trail to the east of the village. Drive to the A515 and turn right as far as the turning on the left to Tissington (estate village and hall, well dressings). Return to the main road and cross to follow the side road through Thorpe (church and cottages, hotel). On across Dovedale (scenic walks), and into Ilam (riverside walks, estate - National Trust property). Turn right and drive through Alstonfield (pub, cafés, costume museum). Left to Wetton and go steeply into the Manifold Valley, then climb to Grindon. Left at the B5053, through Onecote and climb steadily to a crossroads. Turn right and follow the long curving highroad across Morridge to the vantage point of the Mermaid Inn. Bear right at the second fork beyond the inn, down to the B5053 and left into the old market village of Longnor (pubs, craft centre, fish and chips). Follow the ridge road above Dovedale, through Sheen and at the B5054 turn left through Hartington (shops, cafés, pubs).

A tour of the Dark Peak

Around 51 miles
This drive crosses the wild moors of the Dark Peak, contrasting them with sheltered valleys at their foot.

From Chapel-en-le-Frith self-styled 'Capital of the Peak', follow the A624 to Hayfield (interesting village away from the main road; shops, cafés, pubs). Drive on into Glossop (shops, Heritage Centre) and turn right to follow the A57 over the 1680 foot high Snake Pass and down into the lovely Woodlands Valley and Ladybower Reservoir. Turn left at the viaduct and drive along the reservoir road to its end. (NB. on summer weekends and Bank Holidays, the road is closed to cars beyond Fairholmes. A bus operates on this stretch at that time.) Return to the A57 and turn left to cross the viaduct, then right at the A6013 through Bamford. Right at the A625, through Brough to Hope (church, shops, pubs), and right for the Edale valley road. Follow this past the turning to Edale village (national park information, cafés, pubs), and onwards to climb steeply to Mam Nick (scenic car park, Mam Tor, Blue John Cavern). Turn right and follow the A625 alongside Rushup Edge (Chestnut Centre - otter and owl sanctuary), into Chapel-en-le-Frith.

Useful information for visitors

Accommodation

The Peak District provides a wide range of accommodation from luxury hotels to simple camp sites. It is not possible to list them in this book, but detailed up-to-date lists can be obtained through the District Council Tourism Publications, or Tourist Information Centres, *for details see page 185.*

Activity Holidays and Outdoor Instruction

'Artuition'
Forge Farm Studio,
Wootton,
Ashbourne DE6 2GW
Tel/Fax: (01335) 324439.
Art courses.

Bagshawe Cavern
12 Bradwell Head Rd;
Bradwell, Hope Valley.
Tel: (01433) 620540
Caving instruction.

Carsington Sport and Leisure
Carsington Water,
Ashbourne DE6 1ST
Tel: (01629) 540478.
Fax: (01629) 540666
Sailing, sail board and canoe instruction.
Cycle hire.

Countrywide Holidays
Moorgate Guest House,
Edale Rd;
Hope Valley S33 6RF
Tel (0161) 446 2226
Walking holidays in the Peak District.

Crimea Farm, Losehill
Castleton,
Hope Valley S30 2WB
Tel: (01433) 621082
Spinning, natural dyeing

and paper making. Rare breeds farm.

David Matthews
3 Unity Villas, Dale Road North, Darley Dale,
Matlock DE4 2HX.
Tel: (01629) 732445
Outdoor activity courses: rock climbing, abseiling, caving, mine exploration, orienteering, hill walking and team/management development.
AALA licenced.

Denstone Stud and Riding Centre
Hall Riddings, Denstone,
Staffs ST14 5HW.
Tel: (01889) 591472. Horse riding instruction.

Derbyshire & Lancashire Gliding Club
Great Hucklow, Tideswell
SK17 8RQ.
Tel: (01298) 871270.
Fax: (01298) 871207

Derwent Outdoor Pursuits and Training Services
Cromford Mill, Mill Lane,
Cromford DE4 3RQ.
Tel: (01629) 824179
Fax: (01629) 826325
Outdoor adventure training for groups and families.

Edale YHA Activity Centre
Rowland Cote, Nether Booth, Edale,
Hope Valley S33 7ZH
Tel: (01433) 670302.
Fax: (01433) 670243
Residential courses for all age groups. Activities include climbing, abseiling, caving, canoeing and kayaking, walking, orienteering, pony trekking, hang gliding and mountain biking.

Endon Riding School
Coltslow Farm, Stanley Moss Lane, Stockton Brook, Stoke-on-Trent
ST9 9LR
Tel: (01782) 502114
Horse riding.

Gliding instruction
Derbyshire Sports Ltd;
The Old Vicarage,
Wetton,
nr Ashbourne DE6 2AF
Tel: (01335) 310296
Hang gliding courses.

Grindles Pony Stud
Woodlands,
Sir William Hill Rd;
Grindleford,
Hope Valley S32 2HS
Tel: (01433) 631593
Riding instruction.

Ladybooth Trekking Centre
Nether Booth, Edale,
Hope Valley S33 7ZH.
Tel: (01433) 670205
Pony trekking.

Losehill Hall Peak District Activity Centre
Castleton, Hope Valley
S33 8WB.
Tel: (01433) 620373
Fax: (01433) 620346
Courses ranging from art, heritage, photography to outdoor activities.

Moorland Adventure
42 Miler Meadow,
Rainow,
Cheshire SK10 5UE
Tel: (01625) 573615
Caving, canoeing, climbing, outdoor initiative, walking and navigation training.
Family action holidays arranged.

Mountain Activities
70 Dig Lane, Wybunbury,
Nantwich,

Cheshire CW5 7EY
Tel: (01270) 814379
Rock climbing instruction for beginners and improvers.

Northfield Farm Riding and Trekking Centre
Flash, nr Buxton
SK17 0SW
Tel: (01298) 22543
Riding instruction and pony trekking. Two day trail rides.
Disabled welcome.

The Old Furnace Walking Holidays
Greendale, Oakamoor,
North Staffs ST10 3AP
Tel: (01538) 703331
Fax: (01538) 703337
Guided walking holidays in Staffordshire.
Moorlands and Derbyshire Dales for small groups and single people.

Old Vicarage Holidays
Kempshill Cottage,
Alma Rd; Tideswell,
Derbyshire SK17 8ND
Tel: (01298) 872101/3
Guided walking holidays in the Peak District.

Peak Activities Ltd
Rock Lea Activity Centre,
Station Road, Hathersage,
Hope Valley S32 1DD
Tel: ()1433) 650345
Fax: (01433) 650342
Outdoor activity training.

Peak School of Hang Gliding
The Elms Farm, Wetton,
nr Ashbourne DE6 2AF
Tel/fax: (01335) 310257
Hang gliding courses.

Red House Stables and Working Museum
Old Road, Darley Dale,
Matlock DE4 2ER
Tel: (01629) 733583

Horse driving courses for beginners to experts.

Rock, Moor and Mountain

6 Stonewood Grove,
Sandy Gate,
Sheffield S10 5SS.
Tel/Fax: (0114) 2630277
Rock climbing, caving,
orienteering and
hillwalking instruction.

White Hall Centre

Long Hill, Buxton SK1 6SX
Tel: (01298) 23260
Fax: (01298) 25945
Adventure activities and
outdoor instruction for
individuals and groups.

Agricultural Shows, Flower Festivals and Sheepdog Trials

See *Peakland Post* and
other local free
newspapers for dates.

Alstonfield Show, May;
Ashbourne Show,
August;
Ashover Show, August;
Bakewell Show, August;
**Bamford Sheepdog
Trials**, May;
**Biggin Church Flower
Festival**, July;
**Birchover Open Gardens
& Flower Festival**, July;
Bradwell Open Gardens,
August;
**Castleton Garland
Ceremony**, May 29;
**Chatsworth Horticultural
Show**, August;
**Chatsworth Country
Fair**, August;
**Chelmorton Flower
Festival**, associated
with village well
dressings – June;
**Derbyshire Country
Show**, Ashbourne,
August;
**Dovedale Sheepdog
Trials** August;

Edensor Orchid Show,
May;
Eyam Village Show,
associated with village
well dressings –
August;
Flash Flower Festival,
June;
Froggatt, August;
Glossop Flower Festival,
June;
**Gradbach Lambing
Service**, May;
Grindleford, August;
**Harden Moss Sheepdog
Trials**, June;
**Hartington Flower
Festival**, June;
**Hayfield Sheepdog Trials
and Country Show**,
September;
**Hognaston Flower
Festival**, May;
**Hollinsclough Flower
Festival**, May/June;
**Hope Show and
Sheepdog Trials**,
August;
Ipstones Flower Festival,
August;
Leek and District Show,
July;
**Litton Horticultural
Show**, September;
**Longnor Sheepdog
Trials**, September;
**Longshaw Sheepdog
Trials**, September;
**Lyme Park Sheepdog
Trials**, August;
Manifold Valley Show,
August;
**Monyash Flower
Festival**, July;
Onecote Flower Festival,
May;
**Penistone Agricultural
Show**, September;
Rowsley Flower Festival,
associated with village
well dressings –
June/July;
**Wardlow Flower
Festival**, associated
with village well
dressings –
August/September.

Archaeological Sites

Map grid reference
numbers next to the site's
name are there to help
locate their position.
Ordnance Survey maps
have instructions in the
use of these grid refe-
rences. Many of the sites
mentioned are also high-
lighted on tourist maps.

Arbor Low

(SK 160635) Neolithic
circle of recumbent
stones, near Parsley Hay.
Access from small car park
and then by foot through
farmyard. Signposted
from minor road between
A515 at Parsley Hay and
Youlgreave.

Bar Dyke

(SK 247946) Heather clad
embankment spanning
the ridge between the
valleys of Ewden Beck
and Hobson Moss Dike
on Broomhead Moor.
Thought to be a
boundary marker built in
the Dark Ages. Access
from minor road north
west of Bradfield.

Battle Cross – Ilam Hall

Saxon cross in riverside
woodland grounds of
Ilam Hall. (SK131505)

Bow Stones

(SD 973813) Twin upright
stones traditionally used
for bending bows, but
possibly an ancient
boundary mark.

Bradfield – motte and bailey castle

(SK266925) Norman
earthworks north west
and south east of village.
No public access, but
right of way skirts the
north westerly boundary.

Bridestones

(SJ 899621) Neolithic
chambered cairn on
southern flank of Bosley
Cloud. Access from
Rushton/Congleton road.

Bull Ring

(SK 079782) Neolithic
henge with causewayed
entrances. Partly
destroyed by quarrying.
Access from Dove Holes
village hall and
community centre.

Carl Wark

(SK 259815) Substantial
stone ramparts and hut
circles dating from pre-
Roman and possibly later
times. Access by footpath
north west of the Fox
House Inn on the A625.

Cucklet Dell

(SK 215762) Secluded
dale below Eyam Hall
where surviving villagers
met during the plague.
On private land, but an
annual service of
remembrance is held in
August – see *Peakland
Post* and other local
papers for details.
Access by footpath.

Derwent packhorse bridge – Slippery Stones

(SK 169950) Rebuilt
medieval pack horse
bridge that once stood in
the now drowned
Derwent village. Access
from Derwent valley
reservoir road end at
King's Tree, then a mile
of easy woodland
footpath.

Edale Cross

(SK 079861)
Wayside cross marking
one of the boundaries of
the Royal Forest of the
Peak. Access from the
bridleway between

Hayfield and the Edale valley.

Elder Bush Cave
(SK 097549)
Prehistoric cave dwelling associated with nearby Thor's Cave. Access from Weag's Bridge in the Manifold Valley.

Eyam Cross
(SK 218765) Fine example of Saxon preaching cross in the village churchyard that once stood on a nearby hilltop.

Five Wells Chambered Cairn
(SK 124710) Well preserved chambered cairn on Taddington Moor where the remains of several burials were discovered in the 19th century. Extensive viewpoint. Access by permissive footpath from lane end to the north west of Fivewells Farm.

Fox Hole Cave
(SK 100662)
Site of cave dwelling presently under excavation at the northern foot of High Wheeldon. No public access.

Gardom's Edge
Prehistoric Settlement
(SK 273730)
Ancient settlement currently being excavated by Sheffield University and the Peak National Park. Access from public car park near the Robin Hood Inn on the A619 Baslow/Chesterfield road; (SK281721). Guided walks in summer.

Grin Low – Solomon's Temple
(SK 054718) Tower on the site of a prehistoric burial mound. Excellent view point. Access from Poole's Cavern and Buxton Country Park.

Hathersage Church
Little John's Grave
(SK 230815) Well cared for supposed grave of Robin Hood's lieutenant

Hermit's Cave
Cratcliff Rocks (SK 226624) Shallow cave thought to be an anchorite's cell. Crucifix carved on back wall. Close to Robin Hood's Stride rocks (also known as Mock Beggar's Hall). Numerous prehistoric earthworks on hillside above. The ancient Portway track crosses gap between both outcrops. Access from footpath north west of B5056 Haddon/Grangemill road.

Langsett Barn
(SK 211005)
Restored 17th-century aisled barn now used as a national park information centre. Access from car park in Langsett village and adjacent to A616.

Lumsdale – Matlock
(SK 313604) Partly restored water-powered mills in natural setting of Lumsdale ravine. Cared for by the Arkwright Trust. Access from narrow lane linking A615 and A632, one mile east of Matlock.

Mam Tor Hill Fort
(SK 128837) Bronze Age and earlier hut base together with defence works on the summit of Mam Tor. National Trust. Access from car park on the A625 at the foot of the hill.

Melandra Castle
Gamesley near Glossop
(SK 009951)
Recognisable remains of Roman fort. Signposted access through council estate.

Minninglow
(SK 209573) Prominent hilltop clump of trees covering prehistoric burial site. Visible over much of the White Peak. No public access.

Mompesson's Well
(SK 222772) Stone well above Eyam where goods were left during the village's isolation at the time of the plague. See also Riley Graves and Cucklet Dell. Access via the moorland road to Grindleford north of Eyam.

Navio Roman fort
near Hope (SK 181828) Grassy outline of fort beside the River Noe south east of Hope. Access by footpath north west from B6049 at Brough. Nearest car park in Bradwell village.

New Mills Industrial Gorge
The Torrs, (SK 001853) Remains of water-powered textile mills almost hidden beneath the main shopping street. Access via New Mills Heritage Centre, Rock Mill Lane.

Nine Ladies Stone Circle
(SK 249635) Bronze Age stone circle with associated King Stone in attractive birch woodland. Part of complex of barrows and henges on Stanton Moor.

Nine Stones Circle
Harthill (SK 227628)
Only four of the original nine tall stones remain. No access, but easily seen from a footpath between Cratcliff Rocks (see Hermit's Cave), and Youlgreave.

Ossam's Cave
Manifold Valley
(SK 096558) Prehistoric cave dwelling. Foot of Ossam's cliff downstream of Wetton Mill.

Peveril Castle
(SK 150827) Norman castle on hilltop above Castleton. English Heritage maintained. Access by steep path from village.

Pilsbury Castle
(SK 114638) Motte and Bailey dating from Norman times. Explanatory plaques. Access by footpath along upper Dove valley.

Portway
sections of the prehistoric track which ran from the Trent valley to Mam Tor, can still be traced from place names across the Peak District.

Reynard's Cave
Dovedale (SK 145525) Natural cave high above Dovedale where Romano-British remains have been found.

Riley Graves
(Sk 226765) Graves of Riley family who died during the Eyam Plague. Signposted along with others, from the village square.

Robin Hood's Picking Rods
(SK 007910) Twin upright stones thought to mark an ancient monastic boundary.

Roystone Grange
Roman farm and monastic grange (SK 201565) Preserved fields and remains dating from Roman to medieval times. Explanatory plaques and leaflet available.

St Bertram's Well
Ilam (SK 136515) Holy well on the side of Bunster Hill overlooking Ilam. Access by footpath.

Thor's Cave
(SK 098549) Prominent cave dwelling associated with Elder Bush Cave above the Manifold Valley. Access from Weag's Bridge.

Three Shires Head Packhorse bridge
(SK 009685) Scenic bridge over the River Dane where Cheshire, Derbyshire and Staffordshire meet.

Washgate Bridge
(SK 052674) Low single-arched packhorse bridge spanning the infant River Dove north of Hollinsclough.

Buildings and Gardens open to the Public

Bakewell Old Market Hall
Tel: (01629) 813227
Restored 17th-century stone-built market house with mullioned windows and gables. National Park Information Centre, displays and talks.

Open: daily (except Thursday in winter).

Buxton Pavilion Gardens
Landscaped park with two ornamental lakes and children's play area. Conservatory. Restaurant, conference centre and cafeteria.
Tel: (01298) 23114
Fax: (01298) 27622

Chatsworth House and Gardens
Tel: (01246) 582204
One of England's treasure houses, home of the Cavendish family for nearly 450 years. Art collections including paintings by Rembrandt, Veronese, Gainsborough and Freud. Furniture by Boulle and Kent. Finest neo-classical sculpture collection in Britain.

The Garden covering more than 100 acres, contains such notable features as the Cascade, Emperor Fountain, maze, giant rockeries and flower gardens. Farmyard and children's adventure playground. Carriage House Restaurant.
Open: Daily from mid-March to early November.
House and Garden:
Open 11am-4.30pm, in June, July and August, the Garden opens at 10.30am.

Behind the Scenes Days and lecture programmes throughout the year by prior appointment.
Disabled access to gardens only. Three electric scooters and two normal wheelchairs available. Please book in advance.
Farmyard and Adventure Playground:
Open daily mid-March to

late Sept. 10.30am-5pm; (last admission 4:30pm). Adventure Playground only remains open weekends during October and half-term week, 12noon-4.30pm
Park: Free access except during times of high fire risk, grouse shooting, or when special events are taking place.

Dunge Valley Gardens
Windgather Rocks, Kettleshulme, nr Whaley Bridge SK23 7RF
Tel: (01663) 733787
6 acres of garden in a setting reminiscent of a Himalayan valley. Rhododendrons, shrubs, blue poppies. Hardy plant nursery.
Open: daily, 1 April-31 August, 10.30am-6pm.

Eyam Hall, Eyam
Unspoilt 17th-century manor house, home of the Wright family for over 300 years. Concerts and other events including Victorian Christmas. 'Hands on' experience for school children. Craft centre.
Open: end-March-Christmas, daily except Monday, (Bank Holidays excepted); 10.30am-5.30pm.

Fir Croft Alpine Garden and Nursery
Calver Sough
Extensive rock garden and nursery.
Open: daylight hours on most days.

Gawsworth Hall
Gawsworth near Macclesfield.
Tel: (01260) 223456
15th-century half-timbered manor house in attractive gardens. Open-

air theatre with covered grandstand. Regular productions mid-June to mid-August.
Hall open Easter to early October, daily 2-5pm.

Haddon Hall
near Bakewell.
Tel: (01629) 812855
Wonderfully preserved example of a medieval manor house, little altered since the reign of Henry VIII. 16th-century terraced rose gardens overlooking a lovely stretch of the River Wye. Due to the number of steps in and around the hall, together with the distance from the car park, it is regretted that Haddon is not entirely suitable for the disabled, or elderly.
Open: April-September 11am-5pm. Closed Sundays, except Bank Holiday Sundays. Group and school visits by appointment through the booking office.

Lea Rhododendron Gardens
Lea near Matlock.
Tel: (01629) 534380
Extensive collection of rhododendrons, azaleas and alpines in a natural wooded hillside setting. Tea shop and plant sales.
Open: mid-March to end July, daily 10am-7pm.

Lyme Park
Disley near Stockport
Tel: (01663) 762023
Palladian fronted hall in 1,300 acre deer park. Used as Pemberley in the TV production of Jane Austen's *Pride and Prejudice*. National Trust property.
Open: Hall, Easter to end October, 1.30pm-5pm Sat.

to Wed. Bank Holidays
11am-5pm. Park open all
year round.

Market House

Winster near Matlock
Restored late 17th or
early 18th-century
market house in main
street. National Trust
property. Small
information room.
*Open: end March-end
October, daily.*

Tissington Hall

near Ashbourne.
Tel: (01335) 350501
Jacobean manor house,
home of the FitzHerbert
family for 500 years in a
quiet estate village
famous for its displays of
well dressing.
*Open: House and
Gardens, June and July,
Monday, Tuesday and
Wednesday 11am-5pm.
Limited wheelchair access
in the Hall and gardens.
Groups and parties
welcome at other times
throughout the year by
written application to:*
The Estate Office,
Tissington Hall,
Ashbourne, Derbyshire
DE6 1RA

Wingfield Manor

South Wingfield near
Alfreton.
Huge ruined 15th-century
mansion where Mary
Queen of Scots was
imprisoned in 1569.
Outdoor events
throughout the summer.
English Heritage.
*Open all year: 1 April-1
November, 12noon-5pm,
(dusk in October).
2 Nov.-31 March: Sat-Sun,
10am-4pm (closed Xmas).*

As the manor
incorporates a private
working farm, visitors
are requested to respect
the privacy of the
owners, especially by
refraining from visiting
outside official opening
hours.

Bus and Train Services

**(See also Travel
Information)**
For bus and train times in
and around the Peak
District, telephone:
BusLine: (01298) 23098 -
open daily, 7am-8pm
Train services:
0345 48 49 50 – open 24
hours, every day.
Train services link Buxton,
the Hope Valley and
Matlock with inter-city
main lines at Sheffield,
Derby and Manchester.
Scheduled bus services
are operated across the
Peak by: Stagecoach Ltd.
Tel: (01246) 211007

Details of all bus and
train times in the Peak
District can be obtained
by 'phoning Busline on
(01298) 23098, daily
between 7am-8pm.
This service is run by
Derbyshire County
Council, who also
produce the Peak District
Timetable which covers
both bus and train
services in and around
the Peak. the timetable
price .60p, is available at
information centres
throughout Derbyshire.
For bus services in
Staffordshire, contact
**Staffordshire Travel/Wise
on, (01785) 276634.**

Coach Operators

Andrews, Tideswell
Tel: (01298) 871222
Bakewell Coaches,
Bakewell
Tel: (01629) 813995
Ennis Coaches,
Middleton-by-
Wirksworth
Tel: (01629) 822357
Glover Coaches,
Ashbourne
Tel: (01335) 300043
Hulleys, Baslow
Tel: (01246) 582246
Matlock Minicoaches,
Matlock
Tel: (01629) 55522
Slack's Coaches, Matlock
Tel: (01629) 582826

Country Parks and Estates

Grin Low and Buxton Country Park

Tel: (01663) 746222
Woodland footpaths link
Poole's Cavern, Solomon's
Temple and Grinlow.

Heights of Abraham Country Park

Matlock Bath. Woodland
walks and caves.
Children's play area,
restaurant. Access by
cable car from valley
bottom.

High Peak Estate

Edale Valley. National
Trust.
Tel: (01433) 670368
32,000 acres of heather
moor, peat bog and hill
farms.

High Tor

Matlock.Roman lead
workings, woodland
walks, viewpoint.

Ilam Park

near Ashbourne.
National Trust. 84 acres

of rolling parkland beside
the River Manifold.
Secret grottos and
woodland walks.

Longshaw Estate

near Sheffield. National
Trust. Tel: (01433) 631708
1700 acre moorland
sporting estate. Gritstone
Edges. Padley Gorge,
relict oak woodland.
*Sheepdog trials –
September. Visitor
Centre, tea room.*

River Etherow Country Park

near Marple. Wooded
river valley and extensive
naturalised mill
reservoirs.

Tegg's Nose Country Park

near Macclesfield.
Tel: (01625) 614279
Part quarried hilltop
above the Bollin Valley.
Wooded lower slopes.
Discovery programme.
Winter sledging area.
Abseil training by
arrangement with the
Ranger Service,

Craft Workshops and Galleries

The area is rich in
craftsmen and women
who work with a wide
range of materials,
usually by traditional
methods. In most of the
workshops visitors can
see craftspeople at work,
but this cannot always be
guaranteed, so check
beforehand. Their
products are usually
available for sale, and
commissions are often
accepted for specially
made items.

Rosalind Annis Gallery

Hollowgate, Holmfirth.

Tel: (01484) 688774
Landscape and still life
artist.

Booth House Gallery
Booth House Lane,
Holmfirth.
Ceramics and pottery.

Caudwell's Mill and Craft Centre
Rowsley. Tel: (01629)
734374 (mill) or (01629)
733185 (craft centre)
Fully operating water-
powered flour mill, café
and craft workshops
making ceramics, glass
blowing, furniture
restoration, paintings
and jewellery.
*Open: daily March-
January; weekends only
January/February.
April/October 10am-6pm,
Nov./March 10am-4:30pm.*

Chapel House Furniture
Tideswell.
Tel: (01298) 871096
Makers of English Oak
furniture. *Open:
weekdays 9am-5pm.*

Craft Supplies
Miller's Dale.
Tel: (01298) 871636
Woodworkers' supplies.
Woodturning, wood
carving, furniture
restoration and
pyrography courses.
Woodturning
demonstrations and
exhibitions.

Derbyshire Craft Centre
Calver Bridge,
near Baslow.
Tel: (01433) 631231
Largest craft shop in
Derbyshire. Egon Ronay
recommended eating
house. *Open: daily, 10am-
6pm. Closed Xmas and
New Year holidays.*

Derwent Crystal
Shaw Croft, Ashbourne.
Tel: (01335) 345219
Demonstrations and
exhibition of hand-made
crystal. *Open: Monday-
Saturday 9am-5pm;
Sunday 11am-4pm.*

Doll's Hospital
Buxton Road, Longnor.
Tel: (01298) 83894
Repairs to dolls and
teddy bears. Also sell
patchwork fabrics.

Eyam Hall Craft Centre
Eyam. Tel: (01433) 631976
Stained glass, stencil,
knitting and
woodturning, musical
instrument making and
restoration, leather work
and ceramic workshops.

Nigel Griffiths
Old Cheese Factory,
Grangemill, near Winster.
Tel: (01629) 650720
Hand-made high quality
oak furniture.
*Open: Monday-Saturday,
9am-5pm.*

Hope House Costume Museum and Restoration Workshop
Alstonfield.
Tel: (01335) 310318
Costume restoration
demonstrations and
exhibition. *Open: by
appointment only.*

Ashley Jackson
13/15 Huddersfield Road,
Holmfirth.
Tel: (01484) 686460
Watercolours of Pennine
and Yorkshire landscapes.

TC Jones (T/A Frank Pratt)
Church Walk,Wirksworth.
Tel: (01629) 822828
Hand-made and hand
carved-furniture.
*Open: Monday-Friday
9am-5pm, Saturday 9am-*

*12.30pm. Saturday
afternoons and Sunday
by prior appointment.*

Lathkill Craft Centre
Manor Farm,
Over Haddon.
Ceramics, furniture,
stained glass, paintings
and bookbinding. Gift
shop and tea rooms.
Open: daily 10am-5pm.

Andrew Lawton Furniture
Goatscliffe Workshops,
Grindleford.
Tel: (01433) 631754
Hand made furniture to
modern designs.
*Open: Monday-Friday
9am-5pm, Saturday
10am-5pm.*

Longnor Craft Centre
Market Square, Longnor.
Tel: (01298) 83587
Exhibitions and sale of
work by local
craftspeople and artists.
Hand-made furniture.
*Open: March-December
daily 10am-5pm; January
and February, Saturday
and Sunday only.*

Manifold Valley Patchwork
Unit 2, Buxton Road,
Longnor.
Tel: (01298) 83801
Quilt-making and
patchwork courses.
Fabric supplies.

David Mellor
The Round Building,
Hathersage.
Tel: (01433) 650220
Cutlery manufacturer.
Shop. Factory tours.
*Open: Monday-Saturday
10am-5pm,
Sunday 11am-5pm.*

Millrace Glass
4 Greenfield Road,
Holmfirth.

Tel: (01484) 681149
Glass studio.

Old Shop Craft Pottery
High St, Alton.
Tel: (01538) 702065
Decorated earthenware,
stoneware and sculpture.
*Open: every afternoon
and Monday, Tuesday
and Wednesday
mornings.*

Pollyanna Pickering
Oaker near Matlock.
Tel: (01629) 55851
Internationally renowned
wildlife artist. Frequent
exhibitions especially
around Christmas –
see local press for dates.

Rookes Pottery
Mill Lane, Hartington.
Tel: (01298) 84650
Terracotta garden pottery
made on the premises.
Demonstrations of
pottery work.
*Open: weekdays 9am-
5pm; Sat. 10am-5pm;
Sun. 11am-5pm. Closed
weekends in Jan. and
February.*

Sanderson, George and Peach
39 Station Road,
Holmfirth.
Tel: (01484) 684485
Local and national
contemporary art.

Peter and Kate Spencer
The Riddings Farm,
Carsington.
Tel: (01335) 370331
Furniture restoration,
cabinet making,
upholstery.
Woodworking courses.
Small nursery specialising
in herbs, alpines and
unusual plants.
*Open: Workshop, daily.
Nursery, 10.30am-7pm, or
dusk if earlier.*

Trevor Stubley
Hart Holes Studio,
Greenfield Road,
Holmfirth.
Tel: (01484) 682026
Studio and gallery of
distinguished portrait
and landscape artist.

Up Country
6 Market Walk,
Holmfirth.
Tel: (01484) 687803
Designer knitwear.

White Rose Gallery
Daisy Lane, Homfirth.
Tel: (01484) 688408
Paintings and crafts by
local artists.

Cycling and Cycle Hire

Even though the major
through roads of the
Peak District can be a
nightmare and often
dangerous to cyclists,
most of the minor roads
and by-ways are quieter
and therefore more
enjoyable.

The old railway trails of
Longdendale, Sett Valley,
Monsal, Tissington, High
Peak, Manifold Valley
Track and the
Middlewood Way, and
also the upper Derwent
Valley offer miles of safe
traffic free and
reasonably level cycling.
Off road cyclists can also
enjoy the freedom of
many of the old green
roads across the Peak.

Cycle hire centres are
conveniently based near
most of the trails. All
centres have a number of
cycles adapted to people
with special needs,
including tandems, trikes,
duet wheelchair cycles
and the Chevron hand
cranked cycles. The

Chevron which are only
available at Derwent and
Parsley Hay, have been
provided by the
independent charity, the
'Cycling Project for the
North West' as part of
their under the 'Wheels
for All' campaign; see
below for the address.
Peak Cycle Hire Centres
are open all year
between 9.30am and
6pm, or dusk. Some have
limited opening during
winter, but may open
specially for large parties
by arrangement. Details
of the exact opening
times are quoted on the
annual Peak Cycle Hire
leaflet issued by the Peak
District National Park and
Derbyshire County
Council.

Ashbourne
Mappleton Lane,
Ashbourne,
Derbyshire DE6 2AA
Tel/Fax: (01335) 343156
Southern end of the
Tissington Trail.

Bakewell Cycle Hire
Station Yard, Bakewell.
Tel: (01629) 814004
Fax: (01629) 344996
Adjacent to south eastern
end of Monsal Trail.

Bollington Cycle Hire
The Adelphi Mill Gate
Lodge, Grimshaw Lane,
Bollington,
Macclesfield SK10 5JB
Tel: (016250) 572681
Adjacent to the
Middlewood Way. Child
seats and helmets
available.

**Brown End Farm Cycle
Hire**
Brown End Farm,
Waterhouses,
Staffs ST10 3EG
Tel: (01538) 308313

**Carsington Water Sports
and Cycle Hire Centre**
Carsington,
near Wirksworth
Tel: (01629) 540478
Fax: (01629) 540666
8 mile track around
reservoir and country
lanes.

Derwent, Fairholmes
Derwent,
Sheffield S30 2AQ
Tel/Fax: (01433) 651261
Upper Derwent Valley,
partly on surfaced roads
traffic free on summer
weekends, and reservoir
side tracks. Chevron hand
cranked cycles available.

Stanley Fearn and Son
19 Bakewell Road,
Matlock.
Tel: (01629) 582089
Specialises in adult
quality mountain bikes.

**Hayfield Information
Centre**
Station Road, Hayfield,
Stockport SK12 5ES
Tel: (01663) 746222
Fax: (01663) 741581
Eastern end of Sett Valley
Trail.

**Middleton Top Visitor
Centre**
Middleton-by-
Wirksworth,
Derbyshire DE4 4LS
Tel: (01629) 823204
Fax: (01629) 825336
South eastern end of
High Peak Trail.

Oakamoor Cycle Hire
Mill Road, Oakamoor,
Staffs
Tel: (01538) 702049
(Mobile) 0410 399048.
Guided tours can be
arranged for parties of
six or more.Mobile hire
service.

Parsley Hay
Buxton,
Derbyshire DE17 0DG
Tel/Fax: (01298) 84493
Near junction of High
Peak and Tissington
Trails. Chevron hand
cranked cycles available.

Waterhouses
Old Station Car Park,
Waterhouses,
Staffs ST10 3EG
Southern end of
Manifold Valley Track.

Fishing

Izaak Walton fished the
waters of the Dove along
with his friend Charles
Cotton, in 1653. The river
is still one of the best fly
fishing streams in the
country. Not only rivers,
but nowadays reservoirs
stocked with rainbow
and brown trout, offer
sport even to the most
discerning angler. Fishing
in most Peakland rivers is
private, but some hotels
can offer day licences to
their guests. Day tickets
are available at reservoirs
in and around the region.
All anglers must have a
national rod fishing
licence issued by the
Environment Agency.

**Hotels with fishing
rights:**

Grouse and Claret
Rowsley.
Tel: (01629) 733233.
Rivers Wye and Derwent.

Peacock Hotel
Rowsley. Tel: (01629)
733518. Rivers Wye and
Derwent.

Midland Hotel
Matlock Bath.
Tel: (01629) 582630.

Derwent between Matlock and Cromford.

Izaak Walton Hotel
Thorpe, Dovedale.
Tel: (01335) 350555.

Reservoir fishing

Carsington
Tel: (01629) 540478
Fishing from 6 April to 7 October, 7am until one hour after sunset.

Combs
Chapel-en-le-Frith.
Coarse fishing only. Fees collected on the bank.

Damflask
near Low Bradfield.
Day tickets available at the reservoir.

Errwood
near Buxton.
Tel: (01663) 732636
Fly fishing only. Tickets available from Carousel Hardware, Buxton Road, Whaley Bridge.

Ladybower
Tel: (01433) 651254
Trout fishing only from 6 March to 31 October, one hour before sunrise to one hour after sunset. Season permits and day tickets can be obtained from the Fishery Warden's Office. Boats and disabled persons' fishing platform.

Lamaload
near Langley, Macclesfield
Day permits from Barlows, Bond St; Macclesfield, and Trev's Tackle, Wilmslow.

More Hall
Ewden Valley, near Balderstone. Day tickets at the reservoir.

Ogston
near Clay Cross.
Tel: (01246) 590413
Day tickets at the reservoir.

Rudyard Lake
near Leek. Coarse fishing for bream, perch, roach and pike. Tickets from machine at information centre. No night fishing. No fish to be taken away.

Stanley Moor
Axe Edge near Buxton. Fly fishing only. Season, June to October.

Tittesworth
Meerbrook near Leek.
Tel: (01538) 300389
Fly fishing for rainbow and brown trout. Tickets from Fishing Lodge. Closed season November-March. Five miles of bank. Boat hire.

Golf

Visitors can play at any of the following clubs without membership, but check beforehand. Unless specified, all are 18 holes.

Ashbourne (9 holes)
Tel: (01335) 342078
Bakewell (9 holes)
Tel: (01629) 812307
Brailsford, Ashbourne
Tel: (01335) 360096
Buxton and High Peak, Fairfield, Buxton
Tel: (01298) 23453
Cavendish, Buxton
Tel: (01298) 25052
Chapel-en-le-Frith
Tel: (01298) 812118
Chesterfield
Tel: (01246) 566156
Glossop and District
Tel: (01457) 864275
Leek
Tel: (01538) 384767

Macclesfield
Tel: (01625) 23227
Matlock
Tel: (01629) 582191
New Mills (9 holes)
Tel: (01663) 743485
Sickleholme, Bamford
Tel: (01433) 651306
Stocksbridge
Tel: (01742) 882003
Westwood, Leek
Tel: (01538) 398385

Leisure Centres and Swimming Pools

Ashbourne Leisure Centre
Compton, Ashbourne.
Tel: (01335) 343712
Swimming pool and leisure complex.

Bakewell Swimming Pool and Fitness Suite
Tel: (01629) 814205
Indoor pool and gymnasium

Borough Park Leisure Centre, Leek
off Ball Haye Road, Leek.
Tel: (01538) 373603 (pool)
(01538) 373505 (squash courts and sports hall)
Swimming pool, squash courts and sports hall.

Buxton Swimming Pool
Pavilion Gardens, Buxton
Thermally heated indoor pool.

Glossop Leisure Centre
High Street East, Glossop SK13 9DS
Tel: (01457) 863223
Climbing wall.

Glossop Pool
Dinting Road, Glossop SK13 9DS
Tel: (01457) 863128
Swimming pool.

Hathersage Swimming Pool
Heated outdoor pool.

Open May to mid-Sept. only, (closed Sunday).

Matlock Lido and Gym
Imperial Road, Matlock.
Tel: (01629) 582843
Swimming pool and keep-fit training.

New Mills Leisure Centre
Hyde Bank, Road, New Mills SK22 4BP
Tel: (01663) 745424
Swimming pool.

Sherwood Hall
Chesterfield Road, Matlock.
Tel: (01629) 56111
Sports hall.

Wirksworth Swimming Pool
Wirksworth.
Tel: (01629) 824717
Swimming pool.

Market Days and Early Closing

Ashbourne: Thursday (incl cattle) and Saturday, ECD Wednesday.
Buxton: Tuesday and Saturday, ECD Wednesday.
Bakewell: Monday (incl cattle), ECD Thursday.
Chesterfield: Monday (incl Bank Holidays), Thursday (incl flea market), Friday and Saturday. ECD Wednesday.
Matlock: Tuesday and Friday. ECD Thursday.
Wirksworth: Tuesday. ECD Wednesday.

Museums, Heritage Centres and Art Galleries

Bakewell Old House Museum
Bakewell.
Tel: (01629) 813165

Local artifacts, toys, furniture and costume in wattle and daub Tudor cottage. *Open: daily Good Friday-end October, 1.30pm-4pm. July-August, 11am-4pm.*

Brindley Mil

Macclesfield Road, Leek. Tel: (01538) 399332 18th-century restored water powered corn mill containing the James Brindley Museum. *Open: Easter Saturday to end October 2pm-5pm on Saturdays, Sundays and Bank Holidays, and from 3rd Monday in July until the end of August on Mondays. Tuesdays and Wednesdays 2-5pm. Booked parties by arrangement. Tel: (01538) 381000*

Buxton Museum and Art Gallery

Terrace Road, Buxton. Tel: (01298) 24658 Three art galleries showing local and international works. Award winning **Wonders of the Peak Museum** with sounds and smells. Geology and archaeology. *Open: Tuesday-Friday, 9.30am-5.30pm, Saturday 9.30am-5pm. Sunday and Bank Holidays, Easter-end September, 10.30am-5.30pm.*

Castleton Village Museum

Old Methodist Schoolroom, Castleton. Village life through the ages covering farming, local industry and trades, school and customs.

Caudwell's Mill

Rowsley, Matlock DE4 2EB Tel: (01629) 734374

Fax: (01629) 880600 Historic fully operational flour mill run by water turbines. Craft centre and café. *Open: 1 March to 31 October, every day; 1 November to end February, weekends only; (Mill shop open daily) 1 April to 31 October 10am-6pm; 1 November to 31 March 10am-4.40pm.*

Cromford Canal

Tel: (01629) 822831 Preserved section of unique canal. Leawood Pumphouse built to lift water from River Derwent to canal is run, in steam on advertised days. High Peak Junction Workshops at foot of railway incline from canal.

Cromford Mill

Mill Lane, Cromford, Matlock DE4 3RQ Tel: (01629) 824297 or (01629) 823256 Partly restored world's first successful water-powered cotton spinning mill built by Richard Arkwright in 1771. Mill and craft shops, café. *Open: all year, daily 9am-5pm.*

Eyam Museum

Hawkhill Road, Eyam S30 1QP Tel: (01433) 631371 or 630777. Description of how the Bubonic Plague affected Eyam. Paintings and mural representation of the London plague. Geological story of the district. *Open: Tuesday to Sunday 10am-4.30pm. Open Bank Holidays.*

Flint Mill

Cheddleton near Leek.

Tel: (01782) 502561 Restored flint grinding mill. Small associated museum. *Open all year. Monday-Thursday 10am-5pm; Friday-Sun. 2-5pm.*

Glossop Heritage Centre

Henry Street, Glossop SK13 8BW Tel: (01457) 869176 Traces the story of Glossop from Roman times, through the *Domesday* and the Industrial Revolution, to modern times. Victorian kitchen. Art Gallery. *Open: all year (except Sundays, Xmas and New Year); Mon-Sat 10.30am-4.30pm*

Hope House Costume Museum and Restoration Workshop

Alstonfield, near Ashbourne. Tel: (01335) 310318 Private collection of costume and accessories dating from 1842 up to the 1970's. *By appointment only.*

Last of the Summer Wine Exhibition

Scarfold, Off Hollowgate, Holmfirth HD7 Tel: (01484) 681408 Located in Compo's house (as used during the filming), the exhibition covers the 25 years of the series with photographs, memorabilia, etc. *Open all year, every day 10am-5pm.*

Les Oakes & Sons

General Dealer, Hales View Farm, Oakamoor Road, Cheadle, Staffs. Tel: (01538) 752126 Large collection of horse drawn vehicles and memorabilia.*Open: Mon.-Fri. 9am-6pm; Sat.*

9am-1.30pm; Sunday 9am-12noon. Parties by appointment only.

Macclesfield Heritage Centre and Silk Museum

The Heritage Centre Roe St; Macclesfield SK11 6UT. Tel: (01625) 613210. Fax: (01625) 617880 The story of silk manufacturing in Macclesfield. Award winning audio-visual display. *Open: Mon-Sat 11am-5pm. Sun. 1-5pm. Closed Xmas, New Year and Good Friday.*

Magpie Mine

Sheldon near Bakewell. Tel: (01629) 583834 Restored surface works of one of the last lead mines in the Peak. *Open: all reasonable times, but not always staffed.*

Middleton Top Engine House

Cromford and High Peak Railway, near Wirksworth Steam engine relating to the Middleton Incline. *Operated on advertised days.*

National Stone Centre

Porter Lane, Wirksworth DE4 4FY Tel: (01629) 825403 Story of stone – its geology, history, uses, technology and environmental issues. Site Trails over fossilised coral reefs. Gem panning. Educational services. *Open: every day. Winter 10am-4pm; Summer 10am-5pm.*

National Tramway Museum

Crich, Matlock DE4 5DP. Tel: (01773) 852565 Fax: (01773) 8523236

Vintage trams from all over the world operating on one mile of scenic track. Museum and restored buildings. Special events throughout the year (see leaflet). Braille guide books and wheelchair access, plus staff trained to assist the deaf. Specially adapted tram for the disabled.
Open: 10am-5.30pm (6.30pm Sat/Sun/Bank Holidays). April/May daily except Fridays; June/ July/ August daily; September/ October daily except Fridays; plus special holiday opening at Easter and late October.

New Mills Heritage and Information Centre
Rock Mill Lane, New Mills, High Peak, Derbyshire SK22 3BN
Tel: (01663) 746904
Converted stone building with the 'New Mills Story', from pre-industrial history to the growth of the 'New Mill' which gave its name to the town. Children's 'coal mine' crawl. Access to and views of The Torrs industrial ravine.
Open: Tuesday-Friday 11am-4pm; Saturday-Sunday 10.30am-4.30pm (4pm in winter). Closed Mondays, but open Bank Holidays.

Ollerenshaw Collection
Blue John Craft Shop, Castleton.
Tel: (01433) 620642
Considered one of the finest collections of blue john in the world.
Open: every day.

Paradise Mill
Park Lane, Macclesfield SK11 6TJ
Tel: (01625) 618228
Preserved silk mill last worked in 1981.
Open: Tues-Sun 1pm-5pm and Bank holidays except Xmas, New Year and Good Friday. Telephone for winter opening times.

Peak District Mining Museum
Matlock Bath.
Tel: (01629) 583834
'Hands on' story of 2,500 years of lead mining in Derbyshire. Climbing tunnels and working models. Underground visit to nearby Temple Mine. Visits can also be arranged to Good Luck Mine, Via Gellia.
Open: daily 11am-4pm or longer.

Red House Stables
Working Carriage Museum, Old Road, Darley Dale, Matlock DE4 2ER
Tel: (01629) 733583
Working carriage museum and horses. Coach rides and driving instruction. Many of the vehicles have featured in both TV and film productions.
Open: every day at 10am.

Wirksworth Heritage Centre
Crown Yard, Wirksworth.
Tel: (01629) 825225
Story of Wirksworth and surrounding lead mining area.
Open: daily February-end November. 10am-5pm summer; 11am-4.30pm spring and autumn. Closed Monday and some Tuesdays.

Nature Reserves

In the Peak District Nature Reserves and Sites of Special Scientific Interest tend to be run jointly by English Nature and the appropriate Wildlife Trust in the area, either Derbyshire, Staffordshire, Cheshire or Yorkshire Wildlife Trusts. The following list shows the appropriate agency with the major control over the site, abbreviated as follows:

English Nature. E.N.
Derbyshire Wildlife Trust. D.W.T
Staffordshire Wildlife Trust. S.W.T.
Cheshire Wildlife Trust. C,W,T.
Yorkshire Wildlife Trust. Y.W.T.

Agden Bog
near Bradfield, Sheffield - Y.W.T. 6 acres of bog adjacent to Agden reservoir. Bog flora and wide range of bird life.

Baldstone
near Flash - S.W.T. 63 acres of mixed moorland on millstone grit, the habitat for a diverse population of insects and birds. West of the Royal Cottage Inn on the Leek-Buxton road.

Castern Wood
near Ilam - S.W.T. 51 acre reserve of mainly deciduous and scrub woodland on limestone sub-soil.

Combes Valley
near Leek - S.W.T. Deeply cut wooded valley rich in bird life.

Cromford Canal - D.W.T.
13 acres of naturalised woodland and disused canal.

Danes Moss
near Gawsworth, Macclesfield - C.W.T. 31 acres of raised peat moss, haunt of diverse range of bird life, including willow warblers. Ponds attract visiting waders. For safety reasons access is by permit only.

Hillbridge Wood
Taxal - D.W.T. 12 acres of oak woodland with rhododendrons.

Ladybower Wood -
D.W.T. 40 acres partly of sessile oak woodland and heath.

Lathkill Dale National Nature Reserve - E.N.
258 acres of limestone dale and natural woodland.

Macclesfield Forest -
C.W.T. Visiting and resident wildfowl and woodland birds, especially around Trentabank Reservoir where a large colony of herons live. Disabled access path.

Miller's Dale - D.W.T.
Three reserves of 219 acres in total to the south of the Wye. Chee Dale, Miller's Dale Quarry and Priestcliffe Lees. Varied environments based on limestone.

Monks Dale National Nature Reserve - E.N.
149 acres of limestone dale with north-south orientation, so with differing climatic effect to Lathkill Dale.

Overdale Reserve - D.W.T.
45 acre reserve of upland gritstone pasture divided by two streams.

Rose End Meadows

near Cromford - D.W.T.
9 acres of unimproved
meadow with plants now
rare to the Peak.

In addition to the above,
the Derbyshire Wildlife
Trust has a permanent
exhibition at Matlock
Bath Station, the
Whistlestop Centre.

Sailing Clubs

Sailing clubs have use of
the following reservoirs
and may allow day
visitors, but check
beforehand:

Carsington Reservoir
nr Ashbourne. (See also
entry under Carsington
Sport and Leisure).
Combs Reservoir,
Chapel-en-le-Frith.
Dove Stone Reservoir
nr Greenfield.
Errwood Reservoir,
nr Buxton.
Ogston Reservoir
nr Clay Cross.
Rudyard Lake.
Todbrook Reservoir
nr Whaley Bridge.
Torside Reservoir
Woodhead.

Windsurfing is available
at both Errwood and
Carsington.
Watertoys and
wakeboarding are
available at Bottoms
Reservoir, Tintwistle as
well as waterskiing and
windsurfing instruction.

Some rivers and canals
are suitable for canoeing
and kayaking.

Show Caves

Once described as 'so
hollow, the land would
ring if were hit', the
White Peak is riddled
with miles of
underground
passageways. Some are
man-made, the results of
the insatiable quest for
lead in time gone by, but
others are natural,
created by the constant
wearing of water
through the porous rock.
Exploring the natural
wonders of the Peak, or
old lead mines, is only for
the qualified. However,
several caves and old
mines have been opened
up for public enjoyment.
These are listed as
follows:

Blue John Cavern

Castleton,
Hope Valley S33 8WP
Tel: (01433) 620638
Guided tours through a
part-natural, part-mine
where the semi-precious
blue john stone was
mined. Access is down
(and back up), a long
flight of steps. *Open:
daily except Christmas
Day, 9.30am-5.30pm.*

Great Rutland Cavern

Heights of Abraham,
Matlock Bath DE4
Tel: (01629) 582365
Part natural, part mine,
entered via an
interpretive display.
*Open: daily, Easter-end
October, 10am-5pm.*

Nestus Mine

Heights of Abraham,
Matlock Bath DE4
Tel: (01629) 582365
Lead mine thought to
date from Roman times.
Easy access.
*Open: daily, Easter-end
October, 10am-5pm.*

Peak Cavern

Castleton
Tel: (01433) 620285
Only completely natural
cavern in the Peak
District. Part of an
extensive system of caves,
visitors are guided along
level passageways.
Abandoned rope makers'
terraces in entrance.
*Open: daily, Easter-end
October 10am-5pm, daily.*

Poole's Cavern

Buxton Country Park,
Green Lane,
Buxton SK17 9DH
Tel: (01298) 26978.
Natural cave used as a
shelter by Bronze Age
cave dwellers, Roman
metal workers and a
notorious robber.
Longest stalactite in the
Peak District.
16 steps. Partial
wheelchair access. Visitor
Centre.
*Open: March-end
October 10am-5pm daily.*

Speedwell Cavern

Winnats Pass, Castleton.
Tel: (01433) 620512
After a long flight of
steps, visitors are carried
by boat along an
underground, lead
miners' canal to the
'Bottomless Pit' and the
natural part of the cave.

Treak Cliff Cavern

Castleton
Tel: (01433) 620571
Contains some of Britain's
finest stalactites and
stalagmites, rich blue
john veins. Illuminated
throughout. Easy access.
*Open: daily, except
Christmas Day.*

Steam Railways

Scenic lengths of
abandoned railways have
been re-opened by
railway societies to help
recapture the hey-day of
steam hauled trains.
Special events are
organised throughout
the year - check with the
individual society for
details and also current
timetables.

Churnet Valley Railway

Cheddleton Station,
near Leek ST13 7EE
Tel: (01538) 360522
Currently only a mile
long, but up to eight
miles of line along the
mostly road-free scenic
Churnet Valley should
soon be available. Loco
shed, signal box and tea
rooms.
*Operates: March to
September as scheduled.*

Midland Railway Centre

Butterley Station, Ripley,
Derbys DE5 3QZ
Tel: (01773) 570140
Fax: (01773) 570721
One of the leading
railway projects in the
country, steam trains and
specials run on 3½ miles
of track along the Amber
Valley. Heritage site and
country park. Wine and
dine trains, children's
parties, charter services.
*Operates throughout the
year as scheduled.*

Peak Rail

Matlock Station, Matlock
DE4. Tel: (01629) 580381
Use part of the old
Midland Railway
between Matlock
Riverside (above Matlock
Station), and Rowsley.
Headquarters and siding
at Darley Dale. Plan to

eventually re-open the line through Bakewell and Miller's Dale to Buxton. *Operates throughout the year as scheduled.*

Rudyard Lake Miniature Railway
Old Rudyard Station nr Leek. Short length of narrow gauge railway between old station and reservoir dam. Access from car park off B5331.

Steeple Grange Light Railway
Middleton by Wirksworth, nr Matlock DE4 3GA. Tel: (01629) 55123 Close to Black Rocks and the National Stone Centre. Former narrow gauge quarry branch line. Display of mining and quarry railway equipment. *Operates: Sundays and Bank Holidays, Easter-end October, 1-5pm.*

Theme Parks

Alton Towers Leisure Park
Alton, nr Cheadle Staffs. Tel: (01538) 702200 Britain's major theme park. White knuckle rides and gentler entertainments set in landscaped parkland. *Open: March-November, daily 9.30am-6.30pm. Firework displays November. For further details 'phone 0990 20 40 60, or visit on* ww.alton-towers.co.uk

American Adventure World
Heanor, Derbyshire DE7 5SX Tel: (01773) 531521 Fax: (01773) 716140 Adventure rides

surrounding 32 acre lake on reclaimed colliery land. Facilities for the disabled. *Open: daily early April-end October, 10am-5pm.*

Gulliver's Kingdom Theme Park
Temple Walk, Matlock Bath DE4 3PG Tel: (01629) 57100 Chairlift, log flume, mine train, lazy river ride, dodgems, water show and animated bear show in wooded hillside setting. Restaurant. Disabled facilities, but 'phone in advance. Children under 90cm free. *Open: Easter-end October, weekends only April, May, September, October, 10.30am-5pm.*

Tourist Information Centres

Ashbourne T.I.C
13 Market Place, Ashbourne DE6 1EU Tel: (01335) 34366 Fax: (01335) 300638

Bakewell T.I.C
Old Market Hall, Bridge St; Bakewell DE45 1DS Tel: (01629) 813227

Buxton T.I.C.
The Crescent, Buxton SK17 6BQ Tel: (01298) 25106 Fax: (01298) 73153

Chesterfield
Peacock Centre, Low Pavement, Chesterfield S40 1PB Tel: (01246) 207777/8 Fax: (01246) 556726

Glossop T.I.C.
The Gatehouse, Victoria Street, Glossop SK13 8HT Tel/Fax: (01457) 855920

Leek T.I.C.
1 Market Place, Leek, Staffordshire Moorlands ST13 5HH Tel: (01538) 483741 Fax: (01538) 483743

Matlock Bath T.I.C.
The Pavilion, Matlock Bath DE4 3NR Tel: (01629) 55082 Fax: (01629) 56304

New Mills, Heritage Centre
Rock Mill Lane, New Mills, High Peak SK22 3BN Tel: (01663) 746904

The following centres have restricted opening:
Castleton, Tel: (01433) 620679
Chapel-en-le-Frith, For telephone information, ring Buxton T.I.C. (01298) 25106
Edale, (01433) 670207
Fairholmes, Derwent Valley. Tel: (01433) 650953
Hartington Signal Box, No telephone
Hayfield, Tel: (01633) 746222
Hulme End, Manifold Valley. Tel: (01298) 84679
Torside, Longdendale. Tel: mobile 0374 707 353
Langsett, no telephone.
Uttoxeter Heritage Centre, Tel: (01889) 567176

Travel Information

The Derbyshire Wayfarer is a day rover ticket valid on bus and train services throughout Derbyshire. They can also be used for

journeys to/from Derbyshire on services operating between Derbyshire and Sheffield city centre, Macclesfield, Leek, Burton-on-Trent or Uttoxeter.

Useful Addresses

Arkwright Society - The
Cromford Mill, Cromford, Matlock DE4 3RQ

Camping Club of Great Britain and Ireland
11 Grosvenor Place, London SW1W 0EY

Caravan Club
East Grinstead House, East Grinstead, Sussex RH19 1UA

Council for the Protection of Rural England
4 Hobart Place, London SW1W 0HY

Countryside Commission
East Midlands, Vincent House, Tindal Bridge, 92-93 Edward St; Birmingham B1 2RA

Cyclists Touring Club
69 Meadrow, Godalming, Surrey GU7 3HS

English Heritage
PO Box 9019, London W1A 0JA

Heart of England Tourist Board
15 Wheeler Gate, Nottingham NG1 2NA

National Trust
36 Queen Anne's Gate, London SW1H 9AS

Peak District National Park Authority
Aldern House, Baslow Rd; Bakewell DE45 1AE

Ramblers' Association
1-5 Wandsworth Rd;
London SW8 2LJ

Severn Trent Water plc
2297 Coventry Rd;
Sheldon,
Birmingham B26 3PU

YHA Trevelyan House
8 St Stephen's Hill,
St Albans,
Herts AL1 2DY

Well Dressings in the Peak District

Villages are listed in approximate chronological order, the exact dates of which are quoted in the *Peakland Post* and other local newspapers.

MAY

Tissington, Endon, Middleton-by-Youlgreave, Wirksworth, Monyash.

JUNE

Cressbrook (Monsal Dale), Ashford-in-the Water, Mayfield (nr Ashbourne), Chelmorton, Youlgreave, Tideswell, Litton (nr Tideswell), Rowsley, Hope, Bakewell

JULY

Hathersage, Chapel-en-le-Frith, Baslow, Buxton, Bamford, Riber (nr Matlock), Peak Forest, Pilsley (nr Bakewell), Great Longstone, Little Longstone, Bonsall, Stoney Middleton.

AUGUST

Bradwell (nr Hope), Great Hucklow (nr Eyam), Taddington, Eyam, Foolow (nr Eyam), Wormhill (nr Buxton)

SEPTEMBER

Longnor,
Hartington

Wildlife Parks

Blackbrook World of Birds and Animals

Winkhill, nr Leek. Tel:(01538) 308293 Collection of birds and farm pets in a moorland setting. Wheelchair access. *Open: 1 April-end October, 10.30am-5.30pm. 1 November-end March, weekends only, 11.30am-5.30pm.*

Chestnut Centre

Slackhall, Chapel-en-le-Frith. Tel: (01298) 814099 Otter and owl conservation centre. Nature trail. Disabled access to much of the centre. Displays and information. *Open: daily March-Dec., 10.30am-5.30pm. Weekends only in January.*

Matlock Bath Aquarium

110 North Parade, Matlock Bath DE4 3NS Tel: (01629) 583624 or 582350. Large thermal pool containing various species of carp. Indoor aquaria. Hologram gallery. *Open: daily, Easter-end October, 10am-5.30pm. winter weekends only.*

Riber Wildlife Park

Riber Castle, Matlock Tel: (01629) 582073 Breeding collection of mostly European endangered species, including lynx. View point along Derwent Valley. *Open: daily throughout the year except Christmas Day, 10am-dusk.*

What's on - Month by Month

The following are a selection of the main outdoor and other events throughout the Peak. For full details see the national park free annual newspaper *Peakland Post* and other local journals. Well dressing dates are given above.

APRIL

-Flagg Races. Point-to-Point races, Easter Tuesday.

MAY

-Buxton Music and Drama Festival, Pavilion gardens and other venues.
-Chatsworth Angling Fair.
-Tideswell May Markets with street entertainments.
-Bamfod Sheep Dog Trials and Country Show.
-Castleton Ancient Garland Ceremony.
-Wincle Fête and Fell Run.

JUNE

-Archaeological Guided Walks Gardom's Edge
-Tea Pot Club, Flash Village.
-Harden Moss Sheep Dog Trials.
-Chatsworth Flower and Garden Show.
-Bakewell Carnival.
-Rowsley Festival.
-Hope Wakes.

JULY

-Glossop Dale Carnival and Country Fair.
-Birchover Village Open

Gardens.
-Beeley Open Gardens.
-Buxton Festival Fringe Venues around the town.
-Chatsworth Last Night of the Proms, with dancing waters and fireworks.
-Padley Pilgrimage.
-Broomhead Show.
-Buxton Festival of Opera Various venues throughout the town.
-Pilsley Fair.
-Ashbourne Highland Gathering.
-Sheldon Fell Race.
-Buxton Jazz Festival.
-Sheldon Day.
-Leek and District Show.
-Chesterfield Medieval Market.

AUGUST

-Clypping Service, Christ Church, Burbage, Buxton.
-Manifold Valley Show.
-Bakewell Show.
-Ashover Show.
-Macclesfield Forest Chapel Rushbearing Ceremony.
-Dovedale Sheep Dog Trials.
-Ipstones Show.
-Chatsworth Horticultural Show.
-Grindleford Horticultural Society Show.
-Froggatt Horticultural Show.
-The Derbyshire Country Show, Hartington Moor.
-Eyam Carnival.
-Matlock Bath Illuminations, (late August-end October).
-Plague Commemoration Service, Eyam.
-Eyam Village Show.
-Hope Sheep Dog Trials and Agricultural Show.
-Chesterfield August Bank Holiday Market.

SEPTEMBER

-Longshaw Sheep Dog
 Trials.
-Glossop Victorian
 Weekend.
-Eyam Carnival.
-Hathersage Horticultural
 Show.
-Chatsworth Two Day
 Country Fair.
-Longnor Wakes Races.
-North Lees Open Day.
-Hollinsclough Sheep Dog
 Trials and Craft Fair.

OCTOBER

-Annual River Sett Clean
 Up.
-Annual Decorative
 Antiques and Fine Art
 Fair, Buxton.

NOVEMBER

-Dovedale Dash.
-Castleton Christmas
 Lights - late November
 to Twelfth Night (Jan 6).

DECEMBER

-Great Hucklow Christmas
 Lights.
-Matlock Boxing Day Raft
 Races.

Selected further reading

Anderson P & Shimwell D
*Wild Flowers and Other
Plants of the Peak District*;
Moorland Publishing Co,
1981

Dodd, AE and EM -
*Peakland Roads &
Trackways*; Moorland
Publishing Co, 1980

Edwards, KC - *The Peak
District*; Collins New
Naturalist, 1962

Ford, Trevor - *The Story of
Peak District Rocks &
Scenery*; National Trust,
(nd)
*Lead Mining in the Peak
District*; Peak Park Joint
Planning Board, 1983

Frost, RA - *Birds of
Derbyshire*; Moorland
Publishing Co, 1978

Harris, Helen - *Industrial
Archaeology of the Peak
District*, David and
Charles, 1971

Mee, Arthur - *The King's
England - Derbyshire*;
Hodder and Stoughton,
1969

Smith, Rowland - *First
and Last, the Peak District
National Park in words
and pictures*; Peak Park
Joint Planning Board,
1978
The Peak National Park;
Webb & Bower/Michael
Joseph 1987
*The Peak: A Park For All
Seasons* (with Brian
Redhead); Constable, 1989

Spencer, Brian - *Walk the
Peak District*;
Bartholomew, 1987 (and
revisions)
*Best Walks in the Peak
District*; Bartholomew,
1996

Tarn, JN - *The Peak District
National Park - Its
Architecture*; Peak Park
Planning Board, 1971

Dedication

For Matthew, Rosemary, James and Richard,
hoping they will grow to love the Peak District
as much as I have

Acknowledgments

I would like to thank my wife Vera for all her
support and patience while writing this guide,
and for checking my constant spelling
mistakes; Isabelle Lewis for her imaginative
ideas on design and layout, as well as Kay
Coulson for her careful editorial work;
Peter J Naylor for his WEA lectures which
opened my eyes to *Aspects of Derbyshire
History*. Last but by no means least, I
must thank the Peak District people who have
answered my queries while compiling this
guide.

Picture credits:
Front cover top: Chatsworth House; *B. Spencer*
Below: Children's well dressing; *B. Spencer*
Spine: Door-case on the Great Stairs, carved
from Staffordshire alabaster, Chatsworth
House; *Devonshire Collection, Chatsworth. By
permission of the Duke of Devonshire and the
Chatsworth Settlement Trustees.*
Back cover left: National Tramway Museum,
Crich; *B. Spencer*
Back cover right: Chelmorton's preserved
medieval field pattern; *B. Spencer*
All other photographs by B. Spencer.